1996

University of St. Francis
GEN 344.73 L665 4 ed.
Levin-Epstein, Michael D.
Primer of equal employ...

P9-ARX-183

PRIMER OF
EQUAL EMPLOYMENT
OPPORTUNITY

Fourth Edition

PRIMER OF EQUAL EMPLOYMENT OPPORTUNITY

Fourth Edition

Michael D. Levin-Epstein
Associate Editor, BNA Conferences
and Special Projects

LIBRARY
College of St. Francis
JOLIET, ILLINOIS

The Bureau of National Affairs, Inc., Washington, D.C.

Copyright © 1987
The Bureau of National Affairs, Inc.

Library of Congress Cataloging-in-Publication Data

Levin-Epstein, Michael D.
  Primer of equal employment opportunity.

  Includes index.
  1. Discrimination in employment—Law and legislation—
United States.   I. Title.
KF3464.L477 1987   344.73'01133   87-600100
ISBN 0-87179-553-1   347.3041133

Authorization to photocopy items for internal or personal use, or
the internal or personal use of specific clients, is granted by BNA
Books for libraries and other users registered with the Copyright
Clearance Center (CCC) Transactional Reporting Service, provided
that $0.50 per page is paid directly to CCC, 21 Congress St., Salem,
MA 01970. 0-87179-553-1/87/$0 + .50.

Printed in the United States of America
International Standard Book Number: 0-87179-553-1

344.73
L665
4ed

PREFACE

Discrimination in employment based on race, color, religion, sex, or national origin was made unlawful in the United States at the national level with the enactment of Title VII of the Civil Rights Act of 1964. In 1967, discrimination based on age was forbidden by the Age Discrimination in Employment Act. In 1973, handicapped status was added to the list of prohibited considerations, and in 1974 an employment preference was established for disabled veterans and veterans of the Vietnam era.

The result of the passing of equal employment opportunity legislation has been a proliferation of government agencies engaged in policing employment discrimination, burgeoning caseloads, and development of an entire new body of law. As an example of the level of activity in this field, the principal agency involved, the U.S. Equal Employment Opportunity Commission, once had a case backlog estimated at more than 100,000 separate complaints.

This book provides a current, comprehensive overview of the field of equal employment opportunity. Part I lists the many laws, orders, regulations, and guidelines involved, both on the state and local and on the federal level, as well as federal agencies involved in enforcement and coverage of employers, employees, and unions under the various federal laws. In Part II the laws are analyzed according to the type of discrimination involved. The often complex policy and practice issues involved, such as recruiting, hiring, promotion, employment testing, and reverse discrimination, are detailed in Part III. In Part IV there is a discussion of the enforcement and administrative aspects of equal opportunity law.

157,683

This is the fourth edition of the Primer. The first edition was prepared in 1978 by the late Howard J. Anderson, BNA Senior Editor for Labor Services.

The following abbreviations are used in this book: EEO for equal employment opportunity, EEOC for the Equal Employment Opportunity Commission, FEP for fair employment practice, NLRB for the National Labor Relations Board, and OFCCP for the Office of Federal Contract Compliance Programs.

Citations for cases mentioned by name in the course of the discussion are contained in the Table of Cases following Part IV.

In the various parts, references by volume and page are given in parentheses for statutes and regulations as published in BNA's *Labor Relations Reporter* Fair Employment Practice Manual (e.g., 401 FEP Manual 337). There is also a citation to an issue of the *Federal Register* (i.e., 45 FR 74646).

Michael D. Levin-Epstein

Washington, DC
March 1987

CONTENTS

PART 1

EEO LAWS, ORDERS, AGENCIES, AND COVERAGE

1
EEO LAWS, ORDERS, AND AGENCIES

Litigation and enforcement of equal employment opportunity (EEO) obligations can arise under many federal, state, and local statutes and executive orders. Some of the laws under which plaintiffs can sue are relatively new, while others date back more than 100 years. In any discussion of a particular suit, it is important to bear in mind which law or laws the EEO action is brought under, since case law differs according to statute. In addition, it is important to remember that not every civil rights law involves employment discrimination.

FEDERAL LAWS, EXECUTIVE ORDERS, THE CONSTITUTION

Federal laws and executive orders generally have the most far-reaching influence on EEO developments since they are applied on a nationwide basis. They include the following:

1964 Civil Rights Act

The most significant piece of federal EEO legislation is the Civil Rights Act of 1964 (401 FEP Manual 1). Several parts of this Act have relevance to equal employment opportunity, as noted below:

- *Title VI* (401 FEP Manual 1) prohibits discrimination based on race, color, or national origin in federally assisted programs. Title VI does not specifically bar employment discrimination based on sex, but some federal

3

agencies nonetheless have barred such discrimination in their regulations.

- *Title VII*, as amended (401 FEP Manual 11), forbids employment or membership discrimination by employers, employment agencies, and unions on the basis of race, color, religion, sex, or national origin. Title VII was amended by the Pregnancy Discrimination Act of 1978 to prohibit discrimination in employment against women affected by pregnancy or related conditions.
- *Title IX*, as amended (401 FEP Manual 41), deals with the authority of the attorney general to intervene in civil rights cases of general public importance.
- *Title XI* (401 FEP Manual 51) deals with certain miscellaneous provisions, including the right to a jury trial and the prohibition against double jeopardy.

Other Statutes

Listed below are other statutes which are important in the field of EEO activities:

- *Title 1 of the Civil Rights Act of 1968* (401 FEP Manual 61) provides criminal penalties for interference with an individual's employment rights because of his or her race, color, religion, or national origin.
- *The Civil Rights Attorney's Fees Awards Act of 1976* (401 FEP Manual 81) deals with the provision of attorneys' fees under various civil rights statutes.
- *Title IX of the Education Amendments of 1972* (401 FEP Manual 83) prohibits sex discrimination in education programs or activities that receive federal financial assistance.
- *The Age Discrimination in Employment Act of 1967*, as amended (401 FEP Manual 351), prohibits, in general, discrimination against employees or applicants for employment between 40 and 70 years of age, subject to exceptions for employees covered by collective bargaining contracts.
- *The Age Discrimination Act of 1975*, as amended (401 FEP Manual 371), prohibits "unreasonable discrimination on

the basis of age" by recipients of federal financial assistance, including revenue-sharing funds.

- *The Equal Pay Act of 1963* (401 FEP Manual 451) makes it unlawful to pay wages to members of one sex at a rate lower than that paid members of the other sex for equal work on jobs that require equal skill, effort, and responsibility under similar working conditions in the same establishment.

- *The Vocational Rehabilitation Act of 1973*, as amended (401 FEP Manual 501), under Section 503 requires federal contractors to take affirmative action to employ and promote qualified handicapped persons, and under Section 504 prohibits discrimination against handicapped persons in any program or activity receiving federal financial assistance.

- *The Vietnam Era Veterans' Readjustment Assistance Act of 1974*, as amended (401 FEP Manual 521), requires employers with government contracts of $10,000 or more to take affirmative action to employ and advance disabled veterans and qualified veterans of the Vietnam era.

- *The State and Local Fiscal Assistance Act of 1972*, as amended (401 FEP Manual 1001), imposes an obligation on state and local governments receiving federal revenue-sharing not to discriminate in employment on the basis of race, color, national origin, sex, religion, age, or handicapped status.

- *The Immigration Reform and Control Act of 1986* makes it illegal for employers to discriminate against legal aliens merely because they are aliens or look foreign. The provision is enforced by a new special counsel's office in the Justice Department. Employers of 15 or more workers—already prohibited from engaging in national origin discrimination—are subject to new coverage under the legislation only with respect to citizenship status claims filed with the special counsel's office. The bill does not amend Title VII and also bars the filing of duplicate charges with the EEOC and the special counsel.

There also are two important pieces of legislation passed more than 100 years ago that have played a significant role in EEO activity in recent years:

- *Section 1981 of the Civil Rights Act of 1866* (401 FEP Manual 81) has been used in actions to redress employment discrimination based on race, alienage, and national origin. It gives all persons the same contractual rights as "white citizens." Section 1981 does not apply to discrimination based on sex.

- *Section 1983 of the Civil Rights Act of 1871* (401 FEP Manual 81), a Reconstruction Era law, applies to persons acting "under color of state law" to deprive others of federal rights, including employment opportunity.

Executive Orders

There are also several executive orders that have been issued by presidents that affect EEO obligations, as follows:

- *Executive Order 11246*, as amended by Executive Orders 11375 and 12086 (401 FEP Manual 601), forbids employment discrimination based on race, color, religion, sex, or national origin by first- and second-tier government contractors whose contracts are in amounts exceeding $10,000. In addition, contractors become subject to additional requirements to develop affirmative action plans and to take positive steps to eliminate employment bias when they have government contracts of $50,000 or more a year and employ 50 or more workers.

- *Executive Order 11141* (401 FEP Manual 615) prohibits discrimination based on age by federal contractors.

- *Executive Order 12250* (401 FEP Manual 2401) gives the attorney general leadership and coordination authority to achieve consistent and effective implementation of Title VI of the Civil Rights Act of 1964 (401 FEP Manual 1), Title IX of the Education Amendments of 1972 (401 FEP Manual 83), and Section 504 of the Vocational Rehabilitation Act of 1973 (401 FEP Manual 501).

Provisions in the Constitution

Finally, on the federal level, there are several provisions in the U.S. Constitution that affect equal employment opportunity:

- *The First Amendment* (401 FEP Manual 71) guarantees freedom of religion.
- *The Fifth Amendment* (401 FEP Manual 71) states that no person shall be deprived of life, liberty, or property without due process of law.
- *The Thirteenth Amendment* (401 FEP Manual 71) guarantees freedom from slavery.
- *The Fourteenth Amendment* (401 FEP Manual 71) prohibits abridgement of federally conferred privileges by actions of the states.

Regulations and Guidelines

Statutes and executive orders state the general provisions governing a particular aspect of EEO law. However, the "nitty-gritty" of federal EEO law often involves regulations and guidelines promulgated by the various federal government agencies charged with enforcing EEO laws.

Final regulations published in the *Federal Register* are generally regarded as having the force of law, and therefore have assumed an increasing importance in EEO disputes. Promulgation of regulations is often a lengthy and cumbersome process, as opportunity is given for public comment and input by other federal agencies.

In addition to regulations, many agencies issue "guidelines" on various aspects of a particular statute that detail the specific administration and enforcement policy on an EEO issue. For example, the EEOC, charged with the responsibility for enforcing Title VII of the Civil Rights Act of 1964, has issued guidelines on such issues as employee selection, sexual harassment, and religious and national origin discrimination. While these guidelines may not be regarded by courts as having the effect of a statute or regulation, they nevertheless generally are accorded substantial weight in EEO case law.

Various regulations and guidelines are discussed as appropriate in later chapters.

FEDERAL EEO AGENCIES

Many agencies are involved in the administration and enforcement of EEO laws. Federal government agencies include the following:

- *Equal Employment Opportunity Commission*: The EEOC is charged with administering Title VII of the Civil Rights Act of 1964. Under that Act, the EEOC has the authority to investigate and conciliate charges of discrimination because of race, color, religion, sex, or national origin by employers, unions, employment agencies, and joint apprenticeship or training committees. The EEOC is also responsible for administering the Age Discrimination in Employment Act and the Equal Pay Act.
- *Office of Federal Contract Compliance Programs*: The OFCCP, part of the Department of Labor, is charged with administering Executive Order 11246 prohibiting discrimination because of race, color, religion, sex, or national origin by all federal government contractors and subcontractors, and by contractors performing work under a federally assisted construction contract, regardless of the number of employees in either case.
- *National Labor Relations Board*: Although federal policy against racial discrimination is enforced primarily through the EEOC and the OFCCP, issues involving racial discrimination also come before the NLRB under the Taft-Hartley Act. The NLRB has held that the right of exclusive representation given a union under that Act carries with it a duty to represent employees fairly without invidious discrimination. The NLRB also has held that a union that practices racial discrimination against an employee it represents violates the employee's rights under the Taft-Hartley Act and that such a case falls under the jurisdiction of the NLRB.
- *Justice Department*: The Justice Department enforces Title

VII cases involving a state or local governmental agency or political subdivision.

The special counsel's office enforces the antidiscrimination provisions of the Immigration Reform and Control Act of 1986.

- *Office of Personnel Management*: As of January 1, 1979, the Civil Service Commission (CSC) was replaced by the Office of Personnel Management (OPM) and the three-member Merit Systems Protection Board (MSPB). The OPM inherited the personnel management responsibilities of the old CSC, while the MSPB took over the CSC's employee appeals functions. Still another agency, the Federal Labor Relations Authority, was set up to administer the government's internal labor relations program.

- *Office of Management and Budget*: In October 1979, a special oversight unit, designed to monitor the federal government's civil rights activities, was established in the Office of Management and Budget, the agency responsible for developing the President's annual budget recommendations and for supervising management of the executive agencies. The oversight unit reviews the civil rights performance of individual agencies and oversees compliance procedures developed by the EEOC and the OFCCP.

- *Federal regulatory agencies*: The Supreme Court has held that the role of regulatory agencies with regard to the question of job discrimination is a limited one. In *NAACP v. Federal Power Commission*, the Court ruled that the Federal Power Commission's (FPC) role extends only as far as its duty to establish "just and reasonable" utility rates. For example, the FPC has a duty to see that regulated companies do not pass on to consumers costs resulting from discrimination, such as back pay settlements, costs of losing valuable government contracts, and legal expenses. However, the FPC is not empowered to regulate directly and in detail the personnel policies of the companies it regulates, the Court ruled.

STATE AND LOCAL LAWS

New York State enacted the first fair employment practices (FEP) law in 1945; by the time federal legislation took effect, laws in this area were in force in half the states in the country. State FEP laws, often patterned after federal legislation, now are found in most of the states, although the coverage, administrative, and substantive provisions of the laws vary widely.

State laws frequently extend farther than the federal civil rights statutes, however. Employers, consequently, find themselves bound by the more comprehensive requirements of these laws, as well as by the broad ban against discrimination on the basis of race, color, religion, sex, and national origin required by Title VII of the 1964 Civil Rights Act.

In addition to these prohibitions, many states include within their FEP laws bans against discrimination on the basis of age, handicap, and marital status. One far-reaching ordinance, Title 34 of the District of Columbia, prohibits 13 kinds of discrimination, including physical appearance, matriculation, sexual preference, and political affiliation.

State laws often extend more to smaller employers than federal laws do. While Title VII applies only to employers of 15 or more, state legislation may go much farther. In some states an "employer" need only employ *one* or more employees to be covered. Other states make no provision for a minimum number of employees needed to determine coverage.

In addition to FEP laws, many states have separate equal pay statutes forbidding compensation differentials based only on sex.

State FEP statutes are preempted by the Employee Retirement Income Security Act (ERISA) to the extent that these statutes go beyond the scope of Title VII in their treatment of benefit plans, but not preempted insofar as they mirror the coverage of Title VII, the Supreme Court has held. (*Shaw v. Delta Air Lines*)

A more comprehensive discussion of state FEP and equal pay laws, together with text of the laws, can be found in FEP Manual 8A of BNA's *Labor Relations Reporter*.

MULTIPLE FORUMS AND BARGAINING AGREEMENTS

In addition to the laws, orders, and ordinances, collective bargaining contracts also play a role in enforcing EEO requirements. Moreover, the courts have taken the position that the contract and the various statutory remedies are independent. The result is that an aggrieved person may pursue an employment discrimination claim in more than one forum, and if the claim is dismissed in one forum, it may be pursued in another. Thus, the Supreme Court held in *Alexander v. Gardner-Denver Co.* that an employee who had pursued a claim of discrimination through the grievance arbitration procedure under a collective bargaining agreement and lost was not barred from suing in federal court under Title VII. Rights under Title VII are distinctly separate in nature from rights under a collective bargaining contract, the Court said.

2
COVERAGE UNDER EEO LAW

Answers to the questions, "Who is covered under EEO law?" and "Who has to comply with EEO law?" depend on which law or executive order is applicable to the situation at hand.

Coverage is different under Title VII of the Civil Rights Act of 1964, Executive Order 11246, the Vietnam Era Veterans' Readjustment Act, the Vocational Rehabilitation Act, the Equal Pay Act, the Age Discrimination in Employment Act, and Title IX of the Education Amendments of 1972.

TITLE VII

Coverage under Title VII of the Civil Rights Act of 1964, as amended (401 FEP Manual 11), extends about as far as it is possible for Congress to reach under its authority to regulate interstate commerce. The coverage depends on a series of definitions.

A key definition is that of "industry affecting commerce"—the basic test of coverage. The definition is in two parts. First, "commerce" is defined broadly to include trade, transportation, or communication among the states or between a state and a point outside it. Second, the phrase "affecting commerce" is defined to include any activity that would hinder or obstruct commerce.

Under these definitions, the coverage of Title VII is broader than that of the Fair Labor Standards Act, which covers employees "engaged in commerce" or in the "production of goods for commerce." Title VII also has a broader coverage of employers than the Taft-Hartley Act, under which the NLRB has set dollar-value standards for assertion of jurisdiction.The coverage of employers is governed by the following definitions:

- *"Person"* includes state and local governments, governmental agencies, and political subdivisions.
- *"Employer"* includes state and local governments, governmental agencies, and political subdivisions. However, the definition does not include the U.S. government, corporations wholly owned by the U.S. government, or departments of the District of Columbia that are subject to competitive service.
- *"Persons in an industry affecting commerce"* includes in addition to actual individuals the usual organizations that people establish to further a common purpose—corporations, associations, labor unions, mutual companies, joint stock companies, trusts, and unincorporated associations. Moreover, legal representatives are "persons," and so are trustees, trustees in bankruptcy, and receivers.

Number-of-Employees Test

An employer is required to have 15 or more employees to be covered by Title VII. To be covered under this test, an employer must have had the required number of employees on each working day of 20 or more calendar weeks in the current or preceding calendar year. Once this requirement is met, it is satisfied for two calendar years.

Multiple Establishments

Where nominally separate business entities do not individually meet the jurisdictional requirements of Title VII but would do so as a group, the EEOC decides whether to combine them for this purpose by applying the tests used by the NLRB in determining coverage under the Taft-Hartley Act. These tests are: interrelation of operations, common management, centralized control of labor relations, and common ownership.

Successor Employers

One U.S. court of appeals ruled that the successorship doctrine developed under the Labor-Management Relations Act, under which a company that replaces another firm can be held liable for that firm's unfair labor practices, is equally applicable where the replaced firm committed unfair employment practices in violation of Title VII. (*EEOC v. MacMillan Bloedel Containers, Inc.*)

Foreign-Owned Subsidiaries

A Japanese-owned subsidiary incorporated in the United States is not exempt from Title VII by reason of a Japanese-American trade treaty. (*Sumitomo Shoji America v. Avagliano*)

Employees

An "employee" is defined broadly in Title VII as an individual employed by an employer. Although this would appear to exclude applicants for employment, the omission appears to be without significance, since under Title VII it is unlawful to refuse to hire "any individual" on the basis of race, color, religion, sex, or national origin. In contrast to the Taft-Hartley Act, Title VII does not exclude supervisors from the definition of an "employee." Nor are executive, administrative, or professional employees exempted, as they are under the Fair Labor Standards Act.

Government Employees

Title VII extends to state and local governments, government agencies, political subdivisions, and departments and agencies of the District of Columbia. (But see Exemptions Section below.)

Labor Organizations

Title VII's coverage of labor organizations is complicated, since a union may be covered both as an employer and a labor organization, and the definition of a "labor organization" is very broad and complex. To be covered as an employer, a union must have 15 or more employees. To be covered as a labor organization, it must have 15 or more members.

The definition of a "labor organization" includes "any organization in which employees participate" to deal with their employer on the usual subjects of collective bargaining. Coverage is not limited to local unions. It also extends to national and international unions and collateral bodies, such as councils, joint boards, and state or local central bodies.

A union also must be "engaged in an industry affecting commerce" to be covered by Title VII. It may meet this test on either of two bases: (1) by meeting the number of members (15) test or (2) by maintaining a hiring hall or hiring office that brings "employers and employees together."

If a union meets one of these tests, it then is covered if it meets one of these three additional tests:

- It is certified as a bargaining representative under the National Labor Relations Act or the Railway Labor Act.
- It is recognized as a bargaining representative by an employee covered by Title VII.
- It has some formal relationship with a labor organization covered by Title VII as a chartered or joint interest organization.

Hiring Hall, Apprenticeships

The 1964 Civil Rights Act covers joint labor-management committees that control apprenticeship programs or other training or retraining programs. The provisions make it unlawful for such committees to retaliate against any person for enforcing his or her rights under the Act or to advertise or post a notice that indicates any preference, limitation, specification, or discrimination based on race, color, religion, sex, or national origin. There is an exception, however, where religion, sex, or national origin is a bona fide occupational qualification (BFOQ) for employment. This exception does not apply to race or color.

The Act also explicitly makes hiring halls or offices subject to Title VII without regard to the number-of-members test.

Employment Agencies

The definition of an "employment agency" covers any person regularly undertaking with or without compensation to procure employees for an employer, or to procure for employees opportunities to work for an employer. Coverage also extends to the U.S. Employment Service and to state and local employment services that receive federal assistance.

Exemptions

Following is a list of exemptions from coverage of the 1964 Civil Rights Act:

- Religious corporations, associations, educational institutions, or societies employing individuals of a particular religion in all their activities, not limited to their religious activities. But the exemption applies only to discrimination based on religion. It does not apply to discrimination based on race, color, sex, or national origin.

- Persons elected to public office in any state or political subdivision by the qualified voters. The exemption also extends to persons chosen by such elected officials to be on their personal staffs, appointees on the policy-making level, or immediate advisers with respect to the exercise of the constitutional or legal powers of the office. The exemption does not extend to employees subject to civil service laws of a state government, governmental agency, or political subdivision.

- Indians living on or near a reservation (given preference in employment by businesses on or near the reservation)

- Bona fide, tax-exempt private clubs, which are excluded from the definition of an "employer" under Title VII

- Employers otherwise covered, exempted with respect to aliens they employ in foreign countries

- Employees of an employer who is subject to a government security program, where the employees do not have security clearance

Title VII protection is denied to any individual who "is a member of the Communist Party of the U.S. or any other organization required to register as a Communist-action or Communist-front organization by a final order of the Subversive Activities Control Board."

FEDERAL CONTRACTORS

Federal government contractors and subcontractors are subject to EEO provisions in several executive orders and statutes administered by the Department of Labor, in addition to being subject to provisions of Title VII. Coverage under these measures, which additionally bar employment discrimination and/or require affirmative action steps, is described below.

Executive Orders

Under Executive Order 11246, as amended (401 FEP Manual 601), and Executive Order 11141 (401 FEP Manual 615), contractors involved in transactions with the government exceeding $10,000 a year in value must comply with nondiscrimination requirements discussed in Chapter 8. More significantly, however, contractors become subject to additional requirements to develop written affirmative action plans and to take positive steps to eliminate the listed types of employment discrimination within their organizations when they have government contracts worth $50,000 or more a year and have 50 or more employees.

The Secretary of Labor has the authority to exempt an agency from requiring inclusion of any part or all of the nondiscrimination clause (included in contracts to enforce the above-mentioned nondiscrimination requirements) in any specific contract or subcontract when the Secretary deems that special circumstances in the national interest so require. Such an exemption also may be granted to groups or categories of contracts of the same type where it is found to be impracticable to act on each request individually or where group exemptions will contribute to convenience in administering the orders.

Specific exemptions also have been established by the OFCCP covering the following types of contracts and subcontracts: those not exceeding $10,000 (other than government bills of lading); those for work outside the United States with workers not recruited in the United States; those for indefinite quantities not likely to exceed $10,000 in any one year; those for activities an agency head determines are essential to national security where compliance would endanger this. Also exempted are units of a state or local government contractor or subcontractor not participating in the actual work and facilities which the OFCCP finds separate from performance of the contract or subcontract. Contractors working on or near Indian reservations may give hiring preference to Indians in the area. Exemptions may be withdrawn, but only for future contracts and, for advertised procurement, up to 11 days before bids are opened. Multiple contracts exceeding $10,000 are not exempted, nor are an organization's affiliates, subsidiaries, and divisions unless the OFCCP finds the organization is wholly independent of them. Examples of companies considered covered include common carriers transporting goods necessary for performance of government contracts (considered subcontractors), and utilities doing business with the government.

Vocational Rehabilitation Act

Employers with federal contracts worth more than $2,500 are required by Section 503 of the Vocational Rehabilitation Act of 1973, as amended (401 FEP Manual 501), to take affirmative action for the employment of handicapped persons as described in Chapter 8. If the contract is worth $50,000 or more and the company has 50 or more employees, additional requirements apply as specified in Chapter 8.

Vietnam Era Veterans' Act

Federal government contractors with contracts or subcontracts of $10,000 or more are required to take affirmative action as described in Chapter 8 in regard to disabled veterans and qualified veterans of the Vietnam Era, under Section 2012 of the Vietnam Era Veterans' Readjustment Assistance Act of 1974, as amended (401 FEP Manual 521).

VOCATIONAL REHABILITATION ACT

In addition to requirements established under Section 503 for employers with federal contracts (discussed under Federal Contractors above), the Vocational Rehabilitation Act of 1973, as amended (401 FEP Manual 501), specifies in Section 504 other requirements that apply to programs and activities receiving any kind of federal assistance. This coverage extends to employers receiving loans, grants, and other federal monies; services of federal personnel; or federal real and/or personal property. Section 504 prohibits those covered from discriminating against applicants or employees because they are handicapped.

EQUAL PAY ACT

The Equal Pay Act of 1963 (401 FEP Manual 451) was enacted as an amendment to the Fair Labor Standards Act (Wage-Hour Law), and it therefore has the same broad basic coverage and complex exemptions as the Wage-Hour Law.

In general, the Federal Wage-Hour Law applies to employees, not specifically exempt, who meet one of the tests set out below. They may be

- Engaged in commerce, which includes both interstate commerce and U.S.-foreign commerce
- Engaged in the production of goods for commerce, which includes not only the actual production operations but also any closely related process directly essential to the production
- Employed in an "enterprise" engaged in commerce or the production of goods for commerce

The first two types of coverage comprise the "employee test" of coverage—the nature of the employee's work, not the nature of the business, is controlling.

It is the third type of coverage that depends on the nature of the business. If the "enterprise" is covered, all employees not specifically exempted are covered without regard to their individual duties. Dollar volume-of-business requirements under this test exclude smaller employers, but employees of these excluded employers still could be covered under either of the employee coverage tests.

The definition of an employer was expanded in 1966, 1972, and 1974 and now includes state and local workers employed in hospitals, institutions, schools, and "public agencies," thus extending the Act's reach to nearly all state and local government employees. As noted, coverage also has been extended to executives and administrative and professional personnel.

Exemptions

Specifically exempted in the agricultural field are workers age 16 or younger, those working for small employers or family members or principally engaged in range production of livestock, and hand-harvest laborers paid on a piece-rate basis. For industrial and occupational activities the same exemptions apply as set forth in the Wage-Hour Act minimum wage provisions. There are no exemptions for white-collar workers; those originally carried over from the Wage-Hour Act were eliminated by the Education Amendments of 1972, which amended Section 13 (a) of the Fair Labor Standards Act for this purpose.

AGE DISCRIMINATION IN EMPLOYMENT ACT

The Age Discrimination in Employment Act of 1967, as amended (401 FEP Manual 351), prohibits age-based employment discrimination against individuals between 40 and 70 years of age.

While the enforcement provisions of the Age Discrimination in Employment Act parallel those of the Wage-Hour Act, its standards for coverage largely duplicate those of Title VII of the Civil Rights Act prior to that Act's 1972 amendments. (However, in a significant difference, Title VII's coverage includes both employers with 15 or more workers and unions with 15 or more members.) Thus, the Age Discrimination in Employment Act specifies these basic rules on coverage:

Employers

An employer is covered if it (1) is engaged in an industry affecting commerce, and (2) has had 20 or more employees for each working day in each of 20 or more calendar weeks in the current or preceding calendar year.

Employment Agency

An employment agency is covered if it regularly, with or without compensation, undertakes to procure employees for an employer.

Labor Unions

The test is whether the union is engaged in an "industry affecting commerce." A union meets this test if it (1) maintains a hiring hall that brings employers and employees together or (2) has 25 or more members, and it also either (a) is certified as a bargaining agent under the Taft Act or Railway Labor Act, (b) is otherwise recognized as a bargaining agent by an employee, or (c) has some formal relationship with a covered union, such as having charted such a union, having been chartered by such a union, or being a member of a joint council or other organization which includes such a union.

Government Employees

The Act applies to state and local government employees, as well as to federal and private sector employees, the Supreme Court has ruled. (*EEOC v. Wyoming*)

TITLE IX OF THE EDUCATION AMENDMENTS OF 1972

Title IX of the Education Amendments of 1972 (401 FEP Manual 83) prohibits sex discrimination by educational institutions receiving federal funds. Whether the law also covered discrimination in employment at such institutions was a question which was the subject of conflicting decisions in the court system until the Supreme Court reviewed the issue in *North Haven Board of Education v. Bell*. In that case, the Court ruled 6 to 3 that Title IX extends to school employment practices. The Court held that the law's "broad directive that 'no person' may be discriminated against on the basis of gender appears, on its face, to include employees as well as students." Endorsing regulations, originally issued by the Department of Health, Education, and Welfare, empowering the government to withdraw federal funds when a school system is found to discriminate against employees on the basis of sex, the Court concluded that Congress intended employment practices to be covered, even though Title IX does not specifically express that prohibition.

PART 2

FORBIDDEN DISCRIMINATION AND AFFIRMATIVE ACTION

157,683

LIBRARY
College of St. Francis
JOLIET, ILLINOIS

3
TITLE VII: SEX

The attempt to deal with the problem of racial discrimination was the major reason for the development of EEO and FEP legislation; in many cases, the rules against discrimination on the basis of sex, religion, national origin, or age. Prohibitions against racial discrimination are addressed as part of the discussion in Part 3. Other types of discrimination prohibited either by Title VII or by other legislation are discussed in Part 2 and, to a lesser extent, in Part 3.

Under Title VII of the Civil Rights Act of 1964 (401 FEP Manual 11) it is an unfair employment practice for an employer to limit, segregate, or classify employees in any way that would deprive or tend to deprive any individual of employment opportunities or otherwise adversely affect that person's status as an employee because of race, color, religion, sex, or national origin. Title VII was drafted primarily to deal with discrimination based on race, national origin, and religion; the ban on sex discrimination was inserted one day before its passage with little accompanying discussion to clarify the legislative intent. The separate and distinct problems of discrimination based on sex were not covered in the hearings and investigations that led to the passage of Title VII.

It is not surprising, therefore, that the EEOC has had more difficulty clarifying and applying the ban on sex discrimination than it has had in administering any other single provision of the law. Moreover, it has had to relate the ban on sex discrimination in Title VII to the overlapping provisions of the Equal Pay Act when dealing with charges of wage discrimination.

The federal appeals court in St.Louis ruled that a female employee who prevailed on her Equal Pay Act claim that the

27

employer paid her less than a male supervisor who was performing the same job should also prevail on her sex-based wage
discrimination claim under Title VII. The court held that identical standards of proof govern both laws and that the district
court erred by ignoring a jury verdict in favor of the employee
on the EPA claim. (*McKee v. Bi-State Development Agency*)

The courts and the EEOC have wrestled with a wide variety
of issues involving claims of sex discrimination. Some disputes
have involved specific interpretations of EEOC guidelines, such
as sexual harassment. Others have involved far-reaching legal
theories, such as the doctrine of comparable worth. Indeed,
since the passage of Title VII, these and other sex discrimination
questions, including those involving maternity leave and benefits, contributions to pension plans, veteran preference, newspaper advertising, stereotyping in hiring and assignments, marital status, breast-feeding at work, and grooming standards,
have been litigated in federal courts to a degree perhaps unsur-
passed by any other EEO issue to date.

In 1972, the EEOC first issued its Guidelines on Discrimination Because of Sex; following the 1978 passage of the Pregnancy Disability Act, the EEOC revised the guidelines (as
amended, 401 FEP Manual 181) and promulgated a series of
Interpretive Questions and Answers on the 1978 law (401 FEP
Manual 186).

BFOQ EXCEPTION

The ban on discrimination based on religion, sex, or national origin allows as an exception discrimination that involves
a bona fide occupational qualification (BFOQ). The exception
does not apply to discrimination based on race or color. The
EEOC has said in its Guidelines on Discrimination Because of
Sex that the BFOQ exception to the general ban on sex discrimination should be construed narrowly. It would not apply in
these situations, for example:

- A refusal to hire a woman based on assumptions of the
  comparative employment characteristics of women,
  such as the assumption that women have a higher turnover rate than men

- A refusal to hire based on stereotyped characterizations of sexes, such as a belief that men are less capable of assembling intricate equipment or women are less capable of aggressive sales efforts
- A refusal to hire because of the preferences of co-workers, the employers, clients or customers (except where it is necessary for the purpose of authenticity or genuineness, such as the preference for actresses to play female parts)

The courts generally have narrowly construed the BFOQ exception, although perhaps not as narrowly as the EEOC. Leading interpretations include the following:

- In a case involving a state regulation prohibiting women from holding positions as prison guards in all-male facilities, the U.S. Supreme Court held that the regulation was valid because it fell within the BFOQ exception to Title VII. Women can be barred from contact positions in an all-male, maximum security prison, the Court explained, since the possibility of assault on women guards not only threatens the victims but also poses a substantial security risk for other guards and inmates. (*Dothard v. Rawlinson*)
- In a case involving a company rule against hiring women with pre-school-age children, the U.S. Supreme Court said that the test of whether a BFOQ exists is whether it can be shown that the qualification is "demonstrably more relevant to job performance for a woman than a man." (*Phillips v. Martin Marietta Corp.*)
- In a case involving an airline's policy that stewardesses but not stewards must be unmarried, a court of appeals said: "The marital status of a stewardess cannot be said to affect the individual woman's ability to create the proper psychological climate of comfort, safety, and security for passengers." (*Sprogis v. United Airlines*) However, another appeals court disagreed, ruling that the no-marriage rule discriminated on the basis of marital status, not sex, and therefore there was no violation of Title VII. (*Stroud v. Delta Airlines*)

STATE PROTECTIVE LAWS

In the early 1900s, many states adopted laws intended to protect women from the hazards of industrial life by restricting the number of hours they could work per day, the maximum weight of items they could be required to lift, the types of jobs they could hold, and so forth.

In recent years, such laws have been viewed as limiting job opportunities of women rather than protecting them. For example, a law that limits womens' workdays to eight hours may have been adopted to protect them from "sweatshop" conditions but today may serve as an obstacle to the entry of women into executive jobs that often require additional hours of work.

Such laws and regulations conflict with Title VII and will not be considered as a defense to a charge of unlawful discrimination based on sex, the EEOC has ruled. The trend of federal court decisions has been to support this view. Moreover, a number of state attorneys general have issued opinions finding these laws superseded either by Title VII or by state FEP laws. Other states have amended or repealed their protective legislation in this area.

Another type of law found in many states in previous years required that certain benefits be provided for female (but not male) employees; examples are provisions for minimum wages, premium pay for overtime, rest periods, or special physical facilities for women. The EEOC has taken the position that an employer violates Title VII if it refuses to hire a female applicant because it wishes to avoid giving her the benefit required by a state law. State laws giving benefits to women but not to men are not in conflict with Title VII, the EEOC maintains, because the laws can be rendered consistent with Title VII by providing the same benefits to men. The EEOC therefore would find an unlawful employment practice where a company does not provide the same benefit to males as to females, unless the employer can prove that business necessity precludes providing the benefits to workers of both sexes. Upon a showing of business necessity, the employer need not provide the benefit to members of either sex, the EEOC has said.

Adopting the EEOC position, one court of appeals found that a state law requiring employers to pay premium overtime rates to female employees was not invalid, but was to be resolved by paying male employees the same premium overtime rate. (*Hays v. Potlatch Forests, Inc.*) However, another court of appeals rejected the EEOC's approach in a case involving a state law granting an overtime premium for female employees. The court ruled that state law, by providing benefits to women but not men, conflicts with Title VII and is not to be reconciled with federal law by requiring overtime premiums for men. (*Homemakers, Inc. of Los Angeles v. Division of Industrial Welfare*)

MATERNITY BENEFITS AND LEAVE

Discrimination because of pregnancy-related issues was prohibited in 1978 when Congress passed the Pregnancy Discrimination Act amending Title VII of the 1964 Civil Rights Act. The law prohibits disparate treatment of pregnant women for all employment-related purposes. The measure does the following:

- Prohibits termination or refusal to hire or promote a woman solely because she is pregnant
- Bars mandatory leave for pregnant women arbitrarily set at a certain time in their pregnancy and not based on their individual inability to work
- Protects reinstatement rights of women on leave for pregnancy-related reasons, including rights in regard to credit for previous service, accrued retirement benefits, and accumulated seniority
- Requires employers to treat pregnancy and childbirth the same way they treat other causes of disability under fringe benefit plans (In this regard, the Supreme Court has ruled that the 1978 Pregnancy Discrimination Act amendments to Title VII require employers to pay maternity benefits not only to female workers but also to wives of male workers whenever the workers are covered by the employer for other disabilities.)(*Newport News Shipbuilding & Dry Dock Co. v. EEOC*)

The only exception to the mandate of equal treatment of pregnant workers is the provision stating that employers are not required to pay for health insurance benefits for abortion, except where the life of the mother would be endangered if the fetus were carried to term or where "medical complications" have arisen from abortion. If a woman suffers complications from an abortion, medical payments and disability and sick leave benefits for the treatment of these complications would have to be covered by an employer's comprehensive health and disability program.

The drive for the Pregnancy Discrimination Act legislation began in 1976 after the Supreme Court issued its decision in *General Electric Co. v. Gilbert.* In *Gilbert,* the Court ruled 6-3 that a private employer did not violate Title VII by excluding pregnancy from coverage in its disability benefit plan. The Court stated that the disability plan did not exclude anyone because of gender but merely removed one physical condition—pregnancy—from the list of compensable disabilities.

Prior to *Gilbert,* the Supreme Court ruled that a mandatory leave provision requiring a pregnant teacher to leave her job four or five months before childbirth is unconstitutional and violates the Fourteenth Amendment's due process guarantee. (*Cleveland Board of Education v. Lafleur*)

In another case, decided after *Gilbert,* a court of appeals held that a union's policy of limiting temporary workers to 10 days of sick leave may have violated the sex discrimination provision of Title VII, since it has had a "drastic effect on women employees of childbearing age." (*Abraham v. Graphic Arts International Union*)

Many states have passed laws prohibiting discrimination because of pregnancy.

California's law, which was upheld by the Supreme Court as not being preempted by Title VII, requires that employers provide a mandatory four-month leave to pregnant employees and that a woman returning to work from maternity leave be reinstated to the same or similar job. (*California Federal Savings & Loan Association v. Guerra*)

SEXUAL HARASSMENT

The EEOC issued broad guidelines prohibiting sexual harassment in the workplace in 1980 (45 FR 74676, November 10, 1980), incorporating them into the Guidelines on Discrimination Because of Sex (401 FEP Manual 181). Both prior to and subsequent to the issuance of the additional guidelines, courts have generally found that a female employee does have a Title VII claim when she loses her job because she rejected the sexual advances of her supervisor.

In 1986, the Supreme Court issued its first major decision on sexual harassment. In *Meritor Savings Bank v. Vinson*, the Court ruled that

- A Title VII violation may be established even though the victim of sexual harassment establishes no "tangible" or "economic" loss.
- The EEOC guidelines on sexual harassment fully support the view that harassment leading to noneconomic injury can violate Title VII.
- A Title VII violation may be established by proving that discrimination based on sex has created a hostile or abusive work environment.
- A Title VII violation, however, is established only when the sexual harassment is sufficiently severe or pervasive to alter the conditions of the victim's employment and to create an abusive work environment.
- A Title VII violation may be established even though the victim's sex-related conduct was "voluntary." The fact that the victim was not forced to participate against her will is not a defense to a sexual harassment action.
- Evidence of a complainant's sexually provocative speech or dress may be relevant in determining whether sexual advances were unwelcome.
- Employers are not always liable for sexual harassment by their supervisors. On the other hand, absence of notice to an employer does not necessarily insulate that employer from liability.

In its first decision on the issue of an employer's liability for sexual harassment of an employee by non-employees, the EEOC ruled that a restaurant owner violated Title VII by failing to take corrective action once he knew of a worker's complaint that she had been sexually harassed by a customer. (EEOC Decision No. 84-3)

Other decisions on this subject include the following:

- An appeals court ruled that a bank would be liable to a female former employee under Title VII if she proved that she had been fired because she refused her supervisor's demand for sexual favors even though the employer had an established policy against behavior such as that the supervisor allegedly engaged in. The court ruled that the doctrine of *respondeat superior*, under which an employer is held liable, should apply. (*Miller v. Bank of America*)
- An appeals court ruled that an employer that had actual knowledge of a supervisor's sexual harassment of a female employee immediately after her discharge and had failed to take adequate remedial steps was liable under Title VII. An employer need not have actual or constructive knowledge of harassment at the time the advance was made, the court said. (*Craig v. Y&Y Snacks, Inc.*)
- However, another appeals court ruled that an employer did not violate Title VII as the result of a co-employee's sexual harassment of a female employee where the employer took appropriate action to prevent the co-employee from further harassing the female employee. (*Barrett v. Omaha National Bank*)
- A federal district court ruled that an employer's requirement that a female lobby attendant wear a sexually provocative work uniform violated Title VII's ban on sex discrimination. (*EEOC v. Sage Realty*)
- A male supervisor's unwelcome homosexual advances also are prohibited under Title VII, according to one federal district court. (*Wright v. Methodist Youth Services, Inc.*)
- Harassment of a female mechanic was not so severe that it created an actionable hostile environment claim when the only concrete example given of being offensively

propositioned was a senior mechanic's request that she join him at a mall restaurant after work, one court ruled. (*Scott v. Sears, Roebuck & Co.*)

- However, another court ruled that although the EEOC regulations on sexual harassment emphasize explicit sexual behavior, this does not necessarily mean that harassment that is caused by an employee's sex but is not overtly sexual is permitted. (*McKinney v. Dole*)

- According to one appeals court, the offensiveness of the conduct cannot be judged simply by proving that an incident involving sexual remarks occurred, without considering the context. (*Downes v. FAA*)

COMPARABLE WORTH

Comparable worth is a theory for proving sex discrimination in wages that would allow employees to compare their wages to those of other workers performing different jobs with equivalent skills, responsibility, and effort to establish Title VII pay violations.

According to the theory, whole classes of jobs are undervalued because traditionally they have been segregated by sex. In order to break this cycle of sex segregation and underevaluation, which distorts compensation for the intrinsic worth of jobs, the theory holds, Title VII pay discrimination cases must be permitted to be brought without being limited by the standard established in the Equal Pay Act, which provides that jobs must be found to be substantially equal before differing pay rates can be considered discriminatory. This standard is ineffective in reaching the more subtle forms of sex discrimination in wages, according to the comparable worth theory. (See Chapter 6 for a further discussion of the Equal Pay Act.)

Under the comparable worth theory, employees would be permitted to bring Title VII sex-based wage discrimination actions against employers based on a comparison of the value of their jobs to those of other employees who perform work that is dissimilar but that has the same intrinsic worth or comparable worth to the employer.

The courts are beginning to decide the limits on Title VII suits alleging sex-based wage discrimination and whether Title VII claims of sex discrimination in wages can be pursued under the comparable worth theory and without restriction by the equal work standard of the Equal Pay Act. To date, the Supreme Court has decided the question on the narrowest of grounds in *County of Washington v. Gunther,* holding that intentional sex-based wage discrimination is properly the subject of Title VII challenges without restriction by the equal work standard of the Equal Pay Act. But, in *Gunther,* the Court refrained both from specifying any standard or theory and from determining what the limits of proof for showing wage discrimination were, because, it said, in that particular case the county of Washington itself had already established an evaluation system which showed the wage rates for females were too low.

In a landmark post-*Gunther* decision, in a reversal of a lower court ruling, the Ninth Circuit held that the state of Washington lawfully paid employees in predominantly male job classifications more than it paid employees in predominantly female job classifications even though a state-commissioned study concluded that the male-and female-dominated classifications were comparable in worth.

The state "may" have discretion to enact a comparable worth plan, but "Title VII does not obligate it to eliminate an economic inequality which it did not create," the court said. (*AFSCME v. Washington*)

The EEOC and state and federal courts have taken positions similar to that of the Ninth Circuit. (EEOC Decision No. 85-8; *Bohm v. Hartz Wholesale Corp.; American Nurses Association v. Illinois*)

In addition, an appeals court rejected a claim by the predominantly female faculty of the University of Washington that they were underpaid on the basis of sex in comparison with what faculty members in other, comparable schools within the university were being paid. (*Spaulding v. University of Washington*)

OTHER ISSUES

The EEOC and the courts have dealt with a variety of other employer practices involving discrimination on the basis of sex. A number of these are discussed below.

Contribution to Pension Plans

Even though women on the average live longer than men, a pension plan requiring female employees to contribute more than their male counterparts is illegal sex discrimination, the Supreme Court said. (*City of Los Angeles, Department of Water & Power v. Manhart*)

In a subsequent ruling flowing from *Manhart*, the Supreme Court said that an employer-sponsored deferred compensation plan may not use sex-segregated mortality tables for calculating annuity payments. However, this ruling does not apply to persons on whose behalf contributions were made before August 1, 1983. (*Arizona Governing Committee v. Norris*)

Benefits Under Retirement Plans

An appeals court, on remand from the Supreme Court in *Arizona Governing Committee*, ruled that a state retirement system that violated Title VII by providing a higher level of pension benefits to men than to women is not required to equalize prospective benefits for women at the men's higher level. (*Arizona Governing Committee v. Norris*)

In another case stemming from *Manhart*, an appeals court ruled that a state retirement system's retirement plan that uses sex-based mortality tables in calculating benefits for participants who designate beneficiaries is not insulated from attack under Title VII even though the plan provides equal benefits to men and women who select an unmodified allowance and monthly benefits under beneficiary options are based on a nondiscriminatory unmodified allowance. (*Probe v. State Teachers Retirement System*)

Temporary Personnel

A state university did not violate Title VII, an appeals court ruled, by paying female temporary faculty members less than regular faculty members, most of whom were men, since a system of classifying faculty positions either as temporary or regular is not illegal, and temporary employees may be paid less than regular employees. (*Griffin v. Board of Regents*)

Discipline

Personal animosity is not the equivalent of sex discrimination and is not proscribed by Title VII; therefore, the U.S. Postal Service did not violate Title VII when a postmaster suspended a female employee because she failed to follow his instruction, where there is no evidence that he was prejudiced against her or any other woman on account of their sex. (*McCollum v. Bolger*)

Veteran Preference

A Massachusetts law that gives veterans an absolute lifetime preference in public employment was upheld by the Supreme Court. Even though it operates overwhelmingly to the advantage of males and has a "severe" impact on the employment opportunities of women, the Court rejected a claim that the preference law unconstitutionally discriminated against women. The statute was enacted to reward veterans, both men and women, the Court said. The federal government and most states grant extra points to veterans in public employment. (*Personnel Administrator of Massachusetts v. Feeney*)

Newspaper Advertising

Under the EEOC's guidelines, it is unlawful for an employer to run help-wanted ads under separate male and female headings unless sex is a bona fide occupational qualification for the job advertised. Placement of ads under such headings is regarded as an expression of a preference, limitation, specification, or discrimination based on sex. But one court of appeals held that while the EEOC has the authority to issue guidelines on advertising, the guidelines do not have the force of law, and a court would be free to interpret the law differently in any case that presents the issues addressed in the guidelines. (*American Newspaper Publishers Association v. Alexander*)

Stereotypes in Hiring and Job Assignments

If a female employee is performing lower-level duties and consequently is compensated according to a lower pay scale than male employees with similar backgrounds and experience, examination of the reasons for assigning the lower-level duties to the female may reveal that this was based on stereotyped assumptions as to what constitutes "female" work and "male" work. In such cases, a violation of the ban on sex discrimination may be found. Similarly, if a female is rejected for a job because the employer does not believe she can handle the work, the employer's belief may be predicated on stereotyped concepts. If so, a Title VII violation may be found.

A number of courts have had to decide whether employers denying females certain types of work, on the theory that it was "man's work," violated Title VII. For example:

- A court of appeals upheld a height requirement for police officers, even though the requirement resulted in excluding a disproportionate number of female applicants. However, the court struck down a weight requirement with a similar result. (*Smith v. Troyan*)
- An airline did not violate Title VII by its maintenance of a weight program for its flight attendants, despite contentions that the program discriminated on the basis of sex and that it had been discriminatorily enforced against women, another appeals court held. (*Jarrell v. Eastern Airlines*)

Partnership Decisions

A female associate may bring a Title VII sex discrimination action against a law firm that allegedly denied her the benefit of a partnership consideration—a procedure assertedly linked directly with her status as an employee of the firm. (*Hishon v. King & Spalding*)

Marital Status

An employer's rule forbidding or restricting the employment of married women, but not married men, is unlawful, according to EEOC guidelines; even though the rule is not directed against all females, but only married females, it nevertheless involves discrimination based on sex.

Does an employer's rule that a current employee's spouse may not be hired in a similar capacity violate the antidiscrimination provisions of Title VII of the U.S. Constitution? One court of appeals held that the rule did not, despite the employer's inability to prove statistically that this rule—which has substantial discriminatory impact on women—increases production, since the rule plausibly improves the work environment and does not penalize women on the basis of their environmental or genetic background. (*Yuhas v. Libbey-Owens-Ford Co.*)

However, another court of appeals decided that an employer's rule prohibiting the hiring of employee spouses was not justified by business necessity, despite the employer's contention that the rule was needed to prevent employee pressure to hire spouses, where the employer failed to demonstrate how this pressure resulted in lower production or decreased safety, and it did not show that the pressure could not have been alleviated by a less discriminatory rule. (*EEOC v. Rath Packing Co.*)

Another court of appeals ruled that a county's rule forbidding spouses to work as permanent employees in the same department does not violate the Equal Protection or Due Process Clauses of the Fourteenth Amendment to the U.S. Constitution, where the rule bears a rational relationship to its justification, such as avoidance of conflicts of interest and favoritism in employee hiring and supervision. (*Parsons v. County of Del Norte*)

In another case, a court ruled that a county violated Title VII by suspending a newly married female employee for refusing to comply with a rule requiring her to change her name on county personnel forms to that of her husband, where no counterpart rule applied to men. (*Allen v. Lovejoy*)

Breast-Feeding at Work

A teacher in a public school system has a constitutionally protected right to breast-feed her child at work, a court of appeals decided. (*Dike v. School Board of Orange County*)

Grooming Standards

Courts have split on the question of whether different dress codes for male and female employees are prohibited by Title VII:

- A savings and loan association's rule requiring women to wear a uniform but allowing males to wear "customary business attire" of their choice was "demeaning" to women and was "based on offensive stereotypes prohibited by Title VII," a court of appeals ruled. (*Carroll v. Talman Federal Savings & Loan Association of Chicago*)
- But a company requirement that male employees wear ties during working hours is not sex discrimination, even though no similar dress code restrictions applied to women, a court of appeals decided. (*Fountain v. Safeway Stores, Inc.*)

Bias Against Homosexuals

Although Title VII does not specifically mention discrimination on the basis of sexual preference, employees have brought charges of sexual preference discrimination against their employers on constitutional and other grounds. The courts generally have held that employees may not be discharged solely because they are homosexuals. However, discharges of homosexuals have been upheld for other reasons. One court of appeals ruled that a federal employee's discharge for an off-duty homosexual advance was improper. (*Norton v. Macy*)

However another appeals court ruled that an Oklahoma statute authorizing discharge of teachers for engaging in "public homosexual activity" does not violate the Constitution. (*NGTF v. Board of Education, Oklahoma City*)

Discrimination Against Males

Although sex discrimination under Title VII has generally involved charges of discrimination against women because of stereotyped job concepts, state "protective" laws, and the like, discrimination against males also is covered. The refusal of an airline to hire men as flight cabin attendants was found by the U.S. Court of Appeals at New Orleans to be in violation of Title VII's sex discrimination ban. (*Diaz v. Pan American World Airways*)

However, male employees may not sue an employer under Title VII for wage discrimination as a result of their employment in a female-dominated category, an appeals court held. (*Patee v. Pacific Northwest Bell Telephone Co.*)

Sexual Favoritism

An allegation that another female employee's sexual relationship influenced a promotion decision presents a cognizable claim under Title VII, an appeals court ruled. (*King v. Palmer*) The U.S. Veterans Administration was liable for a supervisor's conduct in promoting a female employee on the basis of sexual favors, a federal district court ruled, even though the supervisor's superiors did not know and should not have known about the supervisor's conduct. (*Toscano v. Nimmo*)

4

TITLE VII: NATIONAL ORIGIN

Although Title VII prohibits discrimination on the basis of "national origin," the term is not defined either in Title VII or in other federal statutes relating to job discrimination.

Nevertheless, "national origin" has come to mean the country of one's ancestry—rather than race or color. The majority of national origin discrimination cases thus far have involved Spanish-surnamed persons, a group which includes Mexican-Americans, Puerto Ricans, Cubans, and others whose primary language is Spanish. As a group, Spanish-surnamed Americans—along with Orientals and American Indians—must be classified separately on the EEOC's EEO-1 form, which must be filed by all employers subject to Title VII.

Many of the issues raised in national origin discrimination cases are the same as those raised in race discrimination cases. Like race discrimination actions, national origin discrimination suits tend to revolve around the use of selection procedures which adversely affect protected groups. Thus, testing and seniority are major issues.

One problem considered particularly serious is "covert" discrimination, through which persons of a certain national origin are excluded from employment because of a characteristic peculiar to their heritage, for example, shorter height than the norm or a difficulty with English and/or an accent. In its guidelines on national origin discrimination (401 FEP Manual 201) the EEOC makes the following points:

- Although Title VII provides for a bona fide occupational qualification exception for national origin cases, this exception will be "strictly construed."

- The EEOC will examine with particular concern cases involving national origin discrimination of a covert nature—where, in fact, the individual is discriminated against for reasons "which are grounded in national origin."

EXCLUSION OF ALIENS

Although the EEOC guidelines indicate discrimination against a lawfully domiciled alien amounts to discrimination based on citizenship and therefore on the basis of national origin, which is prohibited, the U.S. Supreme Court has ruled that aliens are not included under Title VII protection. The Act's prohibition on national origin discrimination means exactly and only that, the Court ruled in a case where it found that a job applicant was rejected because she lacked United States citizenship and for no other reason. (*Espinoza v. Farah Manufacturing Co., Inc.*) Nevertheless, the Supreme Court has extended the due process and equal protection clauses of the Fifth Amendment to aliens in public employment areas. (*Sugarman v. Dougall; Hampton v. Wong*)

In addition to constitutional protections, the Civil Rights Act of 1866, which gives all persons within the United States the same right to make a contract, may reach a private employer who excludes aliens, even though Title VII does not. (*Guerra v. Manchester Terminal Corp.*)

Exclusion of Indian Tribes

Indian tribes are excluded from the restrictions of Title VII. Businesses on and near Indian reservations are permitted to follow a publicly announced practice of giving preference to Indians living on or near a reservation.

HEIGHT RESTRICTIONS

Physical restrictions which have the effect of denying a certain class of people who tend to fall below the general norm for height and weight may be ruled as discriminatory if the restrictions cannot be proven to be directly related to the work involved. For example:

- A county was found to have violated both Title VII and the Civil Rights Act of 1866 by requiring that applicants for firefighters' positions be at least five feet seven inches tall, where the requirement eliminated from consideration 41 percent of otherwise eligible Mexican-American applicants and it was not determined that the requirement was job-related. (*Davis v. County of Los Angeles*)

- The EEOC found that an employer's requirement that all employees in the position of baler helpers be at least five feet eight inches tall discriminated against Hispanics. The employer had failed to show that the height requirement was job-related in order to justify its essentially discriminatory effects, the Commission noted in its decision. (EEOC Decision No. 73-0319)

LANGUAGE DIFFICULTIES AND ACCENTS

Unless it is proved that flawless, unaccented English is a requirement for the job, an employer may be found guilty of national origin discrimination for excluding persons who speak with an accent. For example:

- A hotel's requirement of English language proficiency is justified by business necessity and does not violate Title VII's prohibition against national origin discrimination. (*Mejia v. New York Sheraton Hotel*)

- A violation was found where a Spanish-surnamed American employee was discharged because of the employer's unsupported claim that the employee had a "communications barrier" inconsistent with the operation of the business; the EEOC stated that the "clear-communication criterion disqualifies a significantly larger proportion of Spanish-surnamed Americans than non-Spanish-surnamed Americans." (EEOC Decision No. 71-12)

- A company was found guilty of discrimination on the basis of national origin when it refused to consider for employment as a management trainee a Spanish-sur-named applicant who, although otherwise qualified for the position, spoke with "a noticeable Spanish accent." (EEOC Decision No. AL 68-1-155E)

Testing in English Only

An appeals court has indicated that a less rigid business necessity standard might be appropriate in language cases, ruling that a city civil service commission did not violate the Fourteenth Amendment or any of the civil rights of a Spanish-speaking carpenter by giving the examination only in English. The test was job-related, the court said, because the words used would be recognized by persons knowledgeable in the craft. (*Frontera v. Sindell*)

Foreign Language on the Job

Prohibiting employees from speaking their native language on the job, where such restriction is not justified by business necessity, may constitute national origin discrimination prohibited by Title VII. Examples of decisions in this regard include the following:

- The discharge of an Hispanic worker for casually using a Spanish phrase on the job in contravention of a company "rule," which was informally promulgated and not well-publicized, violated Title VII's strictures against national origin discrimination, a federal district court ruled. (*Saucedo v. Brothers Well Service, Inc.*)
- However, an appeals court ruled that a requirement that bilingual employees speak English only on the job is not national origin discrimination. (*Garcia v. Gloor*)

NATIONAL ORIGIN HARASSMENT

An employer is required to maintain a work atmosphere free of ethnic and racial harassment. Sometimes this requirement calls for positive action directed toward those employees who are guilty of harassing others. For example:

- In one case a foreign-born employee was the butt of Polish jokes and "generally derogatory remarks about his ancestry" from fellow employees. By permitting shop harassment of the worker, the employer was guilty of discrimination on the basis of national origin, according to the EEOC. (EEOC Decision No. CL 68-12-431 EU)
- In another case, however, an appeals court upheld a trial court's finding that an employer had not violated Title VII by virtue of a supervisor's use of ethnic slurs directed toward an Italian-American employee who was discharged later for nondiscriminatory reasons. The court said references to the employee as a "dago" were part of a casual conversation which "did not rise to the level necessary to constitute a violation of Title VII." (*Cariddi v. Kansas City Chiefs Football Club*)

5
TITLE VII: RELIGION

Religious discrimination is a far less frequent topic of litigation than race, sex, age, or national origin discrimination. When religious discrimination cases arise, they usually center on two related issues—(1) did the employer make "reasonable accommodation" to the religious needs of employees and (2) was the employer excused from accommodating its employees on the grounds of "undue hardship"?

Both issues have been defined narrowly by the Supreme Court. An employer need not incur more than minimal costs in order to accommodate an employee's religious practices, the Court decided, and it need not take steps inconsistent with an otherwise valid seniority system. (*Trans World Airlines v. Hardison*)

REASONABLE ACCOMMODATION

An employer's duty to accommodate an employee's religious beliefs under Title VII does not require the employer to accept the accommodation preferred by the employee, the Supreme Court ruled. The Court held that an employer meets its obligation under Title VII when it offers a "reasonable accommodation" that removes the conflict between a worker's employment and his religious beliefs. (*Ansonia Board of Education v. Philbrook*)

Several courts of appeals have also been called upon to apply the reasonable accommodation ruling. For example:

- One court of appeals ruled that a union acted lawfully when it requested an employer to adhere to the seniority provisions of a collective bargaining agreement, even though an employee who belonged to the World

49

Wide Church of God would thereby be required to work on Friday nights in violation of his religion's tenets. (*Huston v. Auto Workers, Local 93*)

- Another court affirmed a ruling that an employer and a union made reasonable attempts to accommodate the religious needs of a discharged employee who, as a member of the World Wide Church of God, refused to work the Friday night shift. (*Rohr v. Western Electric Co.*)

- An appeals court ruled that a school district's policy of providing two paid personal leave days for teachers is not an unreasonable accommodation of teachers' religious practices, although this policy might work to the disadvantage of Jewish teachers under certain circumstances. (*Pinsker v. Joint District No. 28J*)

Areas of Accommodation

Most court cases have involved the accommodation of employees seeking to observe their Sabbaths. However, Title VII's ban on religious discrimination covers all conduct motivated by religion and not just situations in which either Sabbatarianism or a practice specifically required or prohibited by a tenet of an employee's religion is involved. (*Redmond v. GAF Corp.*) Another area of litigation has involved accommodating employees who, for religious reasons, seek to maintain a physical appearance or manner of dress which the employer disapproves; the EEOC has indicated that these employees must be accommodated. (EEOC Decision No. 71-1529; EEOC Decision No. 71-2620; *EEOC v. Rollins, Inc.*) Some basic factors the courts consider in determining whether employers have made reasonable efforts to accommodate their employees' religious practices include:

- The nature of the job. If it is specialized or unique, the employer may discharge or refuse to employ a person whose religious practices conflict with its needs.

- The size of the employer's establishment. If the employer is a large company, it may well be required to explain why it could not transfer the employee to a different operation.

- The effects of transferring the employee to a different job. If a transfer means a substantial reduction in pay, the employer may be required to show that no other method of accommodation is possible.
- The employee's efforts in reaching accommodation. If an employee fails to inform an employer of his or her needs or refuses to cooperate with the employer in trying to reach an accommodation, the employee may be considered as having forgone the right to reasonable accommodation.

UNDUE HARDSHIP

The question of how far an employer must go to accommodate an employee raises the issue of undue hardship; in general, the employer must accommodate an employee until doing so results in undue hardship.

Among the effects of accommodation which employers have asserted constitute undue hardship are the lowering of employee morale, the violation of an agreement with a union, scheduling problems, and expense. However, the argument that employee morale will be injured by accommodation has been viewed as inadequate to show undue hardship. (*Roberts v. Hermitage Cotton Mills*)

Here are examples of court decisions finding that the employer did not violate Title VII because of the hardship that accommodating an employee's religious needs would have caused:

- An employee worked in a five-man post office, where the volume of Saturday business required three or four employees to work a full day, and the employee was periodically scheduled to fill in on that day. Following his conversion to Orthodox Judaism, the employee refused to work Saturdays and was dismissed. The court of appeals ruled that the Postal Service did not violate Title VII, since the Postal Service "made a good faith effort to reasonably accommodate the employee's religious observances." The court noted that to accept the employee's demand that he be allowed to work on Sunday, when only one worker was needed, instead of Saturday would result in undue hardship, since it would not alleviate the problem of forcing senior employees to work extra Saturday time. (*Johnson v. United States Postal Service*)

• An applicant applied for a job as a copyreader with a newspaper and stated in his final interview that he could not work on Saturday for religious reasons. The company therefore refused to hire him, and a court subsequently ruled it was not unlawfully discriminating. In order to accommodate the worker's religious practices the employer would have had to assign copyreaders with more seniority to the Saturday shift. This not only would have led to serious morale problems, but also would have cost the employer at least $77 a week in overtime payments, the court found. Accommodating the employee's religious practices would have imposed undue hardship on the employer, the court concluded. (*Reid v. Memphis Publishing Co.*)

CLAIMANTS' REQUIREMENTS

An individual suing his or her employer for religious discrimination first must establish that his or her beliefs are religious within the meaning of Title VII. The EEOC takes the position that an employee's beliefs are protected as religious if they are as "deeply and sincerely held as more conventional religious convictions," and thus holds that atheists are protected by Title VII. (EEOC Decision No. 71-779) The courts have agreed. (*Young v. Southwestern Savings & Loan Association*)

The employee's belief must also be sincerely held. Although some courts have not appeared to question the plaintiff's sincerity, a number have; and one court, after determining that the employee sought to observe a religious holiday because of "convenience rather than conviction," dismissed the case. (*Hansard v. Johns-Manville Products Corp.*)

RELIGIOUS OBJECTIONS TO UNION SHOPS

Some religions take the position that its members should not join unions. This is based on the view that to join a union, which engages in strikes and picketing, would violate the tenet "Love thy neighbor as thyself."

In court, an employee's religious objection to a union security agreement may take two forms. The employee might argue (1) that the requirement to pay union dues violates First Amendment freedom of religion guarantees or, (2) that it violates the Title VII right to be free from religious discrimination in employment. Examples of cases reflecting these concerns are as follows:

- In regard to the first argument, courts have determined that a union security agreement does not violate employees' First Amendment rights (*Gray v. Gulf, Mobile & Ohio R.R.; Linscott v. Millers Falls Co.*)

- In regard to the second argument, a court of appeals ruled that an employer and union that have a union security contract requiring all employees to pay union dues are required by Title VII to accommodate religious beliefs of the employee who claims that such payment would violate his or her religion, unless accommodation would be unreasonable. (*Yott v. North American Rockwell Corp.*)

- In a later ruling, the same appeals court held that an employer violated Title VII by discharging an employee who refused to join a union because of his religious beliefs. (*Anderson v. General Dynamics, Convair Aerospace Div.*)

- In a later case with the same conclusions, however, the appeals court conceded that a union could prove undue hardship if great numbers of employees sought, on religious grounds, to pay the equivalent of union dues to charitable organizations, since the burden on the union and its members would be more than minimal. (*Burns v. Southern Pacific Transportation Co.*)

- Another court of appeals ruled that employees with religious objections to the contractual agency shop requirement must be afforded all reasonable accommodations, including one which might allow them to retain their jobs despite nonpayment of union dues. (*Cooper v. General Dynamics*)

RELIGION AS A BFOQ

In some instances, religion may be a bona fide occupational qualification. When a school, college, or other institution is in whole or in substantial part "owned, supported, controlled or managed" by a particular religion's corporation or society, or if the curriculum of such an educational institution is directed toward the propagation of a certain religion, membership may be required of employees in certain jobs. Such an exemption does not deny any individual Title VII protection, the EEOC emphasized, but merely permits discrimination on religious grounds in selecting employees for certain jobs (EEOC General Counsel Opinion, 10-18-65).

The dismissal of religious discrimination charges challenging a Jesuit-only policy for certain teaching slots in the philosophy department of a Jesuit-run university was affirmed by a court of appeals. (*Pime v. Loyola University of Chicago*)

6
EPA: Sex

The Equal Pay Act of 1963 (401 FEP Manual 451), an amendment to the Fair Labor Standards Act, makes it illegal to discriminate on the basis of sex in paying wages for equal work on jobs which require equal skill, effort, and responsibility under similar working conditions. Enacted pursuant to the commerce clause of the Constitution, the Act was based on a congressional finding that sex-based differentials in wages have a substantial adverse impact on interstate commerce.

The Act establishes exceptions for wage differentials based on seniority or merit system, or a system which measures earnings by quantity or quality of production, or on "any other factor other than sex." In case of conflict, federal law takes precedence over state law.

Unlike Title VII, the Equal Pay Act is limited to the discrimination in wages and does not apply to discrimination in hiring, firing, promotion, or to other types of discrimination. There is an overlap between Title VII and the Equal Pay Act, and Title VII provides that any differential permitted under the Equal Pay Act shall not constitute a violation of Title VII. However, as noted in the explanation of the comparable worth theory in Chapter 3, the Supreme Court has found that the overlap does not mean the equal work concept of the Equal Pay Act is incorporated into Title VII as well. The Court has returned cases brought under Title VII to trial courts for consideration of whether Title VII discrimination may be found based on analyses of job comparability that are broader than the equality standard of the Equal Pay Act.

When the EEOC assumed enforcement responsibility for the Equal Pay Act from the Department of Labor on July 1,

1979, it declined to adopt the Interpretative Bulletin of the Labor Department's Wage and Hour Administrator (401 FEP Manual 461) as its own interpretation of the Act. However, the EEOC noted that until it issues its own final interpretations, employers may "continue to rely on existing interpretations and opinions of the Wage and Hour Administrator to the extent that they are not inconsistent with the statutory revisions and judicial interpretations." On September 1, 1981, the EEOC published proposed interpretive regulations on the Equal Pay Act (401 FEP Manual 325); when finally adopted, they will supersede those of the Wage and Hour Administrator.

The actual wording of the relevant part of the Act establishing the equal pay standard makes it unlawful for an employer to pay wages "at a rate less than the rate at which he pays wages to employees of the opposite sex in such establishments for equal work on jobs the performance of which require equal skill, effort, and responsibility, and which are performed under similar working conditions." Thus, skill, effort, responsibility, and working conditions are made tests of equality of work. (*Brennan v. Owensboro-Daviess County Hospital*) In this regard, the crucial question is not whether employees of one sex possess additional training or skills, but whether the nature of the duties actually performed requires or utilizes those additional skills. (*Peltier v. City of Fargo*) Thus, in several cases, the absence of a bona fide training program has caused the courts to reject the contention that men could be paid more than women performing comparable jobs because the men were management trainees. (*Hodgson v. Security National Bank; Hodgson v. Behrens Drug Co.*)

EXCEPTIONS

The law provides for exceptions to its coverage for wage differentials:
- Paid pursuant to a seniority system
- Paid pursuant to a merit system
- Paid pursuant to a system which measures earnings by quantity or quality of production
- Paid pursuant to any factor other than sex

These four specific exceptions are not restricted to formal systems or written plans. Informal or unwritten plans may qualify if it can be demonstrated that the standards have been applied pursuant to an established plan whose terms have been communicated to the employees.

Generally, if applied without distinction to employees of both sexes, shift differentials, incentive payments, production bonuses, performance and longevity raises, and the like do not present equal pay problems.

DEFINITIONS

Many of the terms in the Equal Pay Act have been elaborated on through various court decisions. A discussion of some of these terms and related decisions follows.

"Equal Work"

Various courts of appeals have ruled on the issue of what constitutes "equal work":

- The work performed by a predominantly male work force of a university in the "heavy" cleaner classification is not substantially equal to work by females employed in the "light" cleaner classification, one court ruled. (*Walker v. Columbia University*)
- In a ruling hailed by the Wage-Hour Administrator as a landmark decision, women employees performing the same basic work as their male counterparts—but receiving 10 percent less pay—were awarded $250,000 in back wages by a court. Both sexes had the same basic duties, but male workers, who occasionally did heavier work, were paid more per hour than female employees. However, the additional work sometimes required of the male employees was in a classification that had virtually the same lower pay rate that the females earned. The employer's lower wage rate for women "clearly appears to have been to keep women in an subordinate role" and the wage differential was based on an "artificially created job classification," the court ruled. (*Schultz v. Wheaton Glass Co.*)

● A bank was found to be in violation of the "substantially equal" provision of the EPA when it paid male tellers more than female tellers. The extra duties of the male tellers were not significant enough to justify a wage differential, the court concluded. (*Hodgson v. American Bank of Commerce*)

"Equal Skill"

Whether two jobs require equal skill depends upon the experience, training, education, and ability required in the performance of the job. In hospital cases, the courts generally have found the work of female nursing aides and male orderlies to be "equal" under the Act.

"Equal Effort"

A number of cases comparing two jobs focus on the question of equality of effort. A test that is widely cited was set forth in *Hodgson v. Brookhaven General Hospital.* Jobs, the court said, do not entail equal effort if the more highly paid job involves additional tasks which (1) require extra effort, (2) consume a significant amount of the time of all those whose pay differentials are to be justified in terms of them, and (3) are of an economic value commensurate with the pay differential.

"Equal Responsibility"

Responsibility involves the degree of accountability required, with the emphasis on the importance of the job obligation. For example, a differential may be justified for one among a group of employees who is required to assume supervisory responsibilities in the absence of a regular supervisor, or for one among a group of sales clerks who is designated to determine whether to accept customers' personal checks. But minor differences, such as the responsibility for turning out the lights or locking up at the end of the day, do not justify a pay differential.

"Similar Working Conditions"

A practical judgment must be made to determine whether differences in working conditions are of a kind meriting consideration in setting wage levels. The mere fact that jobs are in different departments will not justify a pay differential. If, however, some employees do the majority of their work outside the establishment, while others do most of their work inside, the working conditions would appear to be dissimilar.

The Supreme Court found a glass company in violation of the Act when it paid male inspectors on the night shift a higher base wage than it paid female inspectors working days and doing the same job. The pay differentials, the Court found, had their origin in an era when only higher wages could induce men to perform what was termed "women's work." (*Corning Glass Works v. Brennan*)

Factors Other Than Sex

One court of appeals has pointed out that the provision of the Act allowing a differential in pay to workers of different sexes based on "any other factor other than sex" does not require that such factors be job-related or typically used in setting wage scales. It upheld higher pay for salespersons in the men's clothing department than for those in the women's clothing department. The distinction was based on overwhelming evidence that the men's department was more profitable than the women's department. (*Hodgson v. Robert Hall Clothes*)

The Supreme Court has ruled that the EPA's prohibitions do not make it unlawful for an employer to determine funding requirements for an establishment's benefit plan by considering the composition of the entire work force. (*City of Los Angeles v. Manhart*)

ELIMINATING DIFFERENTIALS

Wage differentials based on sex must be eliminated by raising the pay of the lower-rated employees, not by reducing the pay of the higher-rated employee. The law specifically provides that "an employer who is paying a wage differential in violation of this subsection shall not, in order to comply with the provisions of this subsection, reduce the wage rate of any employees."

Opening up to women a category of higher paying jobs previously closed to them does not cure existing pay discrimination, the Supreme Court has ruled. (*Corning Glass Works v. Brennan*)

Female employees, who, in violation of the EPA, are paid less than male employees doing comparable work and possessing comparable seniority and education should be paid the difference in what they were paid, but where an "individualized" approach is not feasible, the female's wages should be compared with the average salary paid to male employees doing comparable work. (*EEOC v. Liggett & Myers, Inc.*)

EFFECT OF STATE LAWS

A number of states have adopted equal pay laws. Where both the federal and state laws apply, the federal equal pay standard is controlling. But the federal standard does not excuse "noncompliance with any state or other law establishing equal pay standards higher than the equal pay standards" provided by federal law.

If, as a result of a state law, women employees must be paid overtime premiums for hours worked in excess of a prescribed maximum workday or workweek, the employer must pay men who perform equal work in the same establishment the same overtime premiums when they work such excess hours.

7
ADEA: AGE

The Age Discrimination in Employment Act of 1967, as amended (401 FEP Manual 351), prohibits job discrimination against workers who are 40 years of age or older. Its stated purpose is "to promote the employment of older persons based on their ability rather than age; to prohibit arbitrary age discrimination in employment; to help employers and workers find ways of meeting problems arising from the impact of age on employment."

The law applies to all private employers with 20 or more employees, state and local governments, employment agencies serving covered employers, and labor unions with 25 or more members. Employment agencies are prohibited from refusing to refer individuals for employment because of age, and from classifying or referring for employment on the basis of age. Unions are forbidden from excluding or expelling individuals from membership on the basis of age.

Under the 1986 amendments to the Act, the mandatory retirement age of 70 was lifted, effective January 1, 1987. Under the 1978 amendments to the Act, the permissible mandatory age was raised from 65 to 70 for most private sector employees, effective January 1, 1979. The 1978 amendments also removed the upper age limit of 70 for retirement of federal workers, effective September 30, 1978.

Until July 1, 1979, the Labor Department administered the Act, but enforcement now rests with the EEOC, which issued its own interpretations of the Act in September 1981 (401 FEP Manual 331), basically paralleling those issued previously by the Labor Department.

A separate statute—the Age Discrimination Act of 1975 (401 FEP Manual 371)—extends the prohibitions against age discrimination to recipients of federal assistance, including recipients of federal revenue-sharing funds.

See Chapter 8 for further information on ADEA provisions applying to employment agencies, unions, and federal workers.

MAJOR PROVISIONS

Prohibitions of the ADEA parallel prohibitions of Title VII. Under the Act, private employers of 20 or more persons are forbidden

- To fail or refuse to hire, to discharge, or otherwise to discriminate against any individual with respect to compensation, terms, conditions, or privileges of employment because of such individual's age
- To limit, segregate, or classify an employee in any way that would deprive such employee of job opportunities or would adversely affect employment status because of age
- To reduce the wage rate of an employee in order to comply with the Act.
- To indicate any "preference, limitation, specification, or discrimination" based on age in any notices or advertisements for employment
- To operate a seniority system or employee benefit plan that requires or permits the involuntary retirement of an employee.

The law provides that if a collective bargaining agreement that was in effect on June 30, 1986, contains provisions permitting forced retirement after age 70, the effective date of the ADEA change would be delayed until the agreement expires or until January 1, 1990, whichever occurs first.

SPECIFIC PROHIBITIONS

Help-Wanted Ads

No indication of a preference based on age may be included in a help-wanted ad, the EEOC states in its interpretations of the Age Discrimination in Employment Act. The ban includes such terms as "age 25 to 35" or "under 40," or descriptive words such as "young," "boy," or "girl." Such a restriction, however, does not bar specifying a minimum age that is less than 40. Thus, an ad stating "not under 18" or "under 35" would be within the provisions of the Act.

The Labor Department's prior interpretation—identical to the EEOC's current one—was litigated in the courts with mixed results:

- An employments agency's help-wanted advertisements directed to "recent graduates" did not automatically violate the Age Discrimination in Employment Act, according to a court of appeals. When the ads are part of a general invitation to a specific class of prospective customers coming into a job market at a particular time of the year to use the agency's services, the Act is not violated, the court ruled. However, if used in reference to a specific job opportunity, use of the phrase violates the Act because it implies that older persons need not apply. Contrary to the Labor Department's position, the court held, "trigger words" such as "returning veterans" and "recent college grad" are not discriminatory per se; the effect is determined by context rather than by words. (*Hodgson v. Approved Personnel Service, Inc.*)

- In another case, where an employer ran an advertisement seeking "college students," "girls," "boys," and "June graduates" to work for it, a federal district court found no illegal discrimination. "There is nothing in the Act that authorizes the Secretary of Labor to prohibit employers from encouraging young persons to turn from idleness to useful endeavor," said the court. (*Brennan v. Paragon Employment Agency*)

Hiring

An employer may ask a prospective employee to give his or her date of birth or "state age" on job applications, as long as the intent is not discriminatory. However, such inquiries will be "closely scrutinized," according to the EEOC interpretations, and it is suggested that employers, agencies, and unions specifically note on such applications that the request is not made for a discriminatory purpose.

Employment Testing

Tests for employment and promotion, as such, are not prohibited by the Act, provided they are validated tests that are (1) specifically related to the requirements of the job, (2) fair and reasonable, (3) administered in good faith and without discrimination on the basis of age, and (4) properly evaluated.

EXCEPTIONS AND EXEMPTIONS

The Act makes exceptions for preferential treatment on the basis of age, as long as it is based on one or more of the following:

- A "bona fide occupational qualification" that is reasonably necessary to the normal operation of business
- A differentiation based on reasonable factors other than age
- Discharge or discipline of an individual for good cause

Age limitations for entry into bona fide apprenticeship programs are not prohibited by the ADEA.

BFOQ Exception

An employer will not be in violation of the Act where age classification or preference is based on a bona fide occupational qualification (BFOQ). However, the BFOQ exception is narrowly construed. Here are some examples the Wage-Hour Administrator saw as possible BFOQ situations, in the interpretations now superseded by the more general EEOC guidelines:

- Actors required for youthful or elderly roles
- Persons used to advertise or promote the sale of products designed for youthful or elderly consumers

However, BFOQ claims based on physical requirements generally were held invalid by the Administrator when the Labor Department interpretations were still in effect. An age limit on construction workers was not within the Act's guidelines, an opinion letter noted; it would not be correct "to conclude that every individual above a chosen age limit is physically unable to perform the vigorous work," the letter stated.

Effect of Federal Statutory and Regulatory Requirements

The Wage-Hour administration, followed by the EEOC, regarded federal requirements that impose a compulsory age limitation, such as the Federal Aviation Agency regulation setting a ceiling of age 60 for airline pilots, as evidence indicating a possible BFOQ exception. Two courts of appeal however, have differed on the question of whether an airline's age limitation for pilots were BFOQs. (*Smallwood v. United Airlines; Murnane v. American Airlines*) An important issue may be the congruity between the occupation covered by the federal rule and occupation affected by the ADEA. (*EEOC v. El Paso Natural Gas Co.*)

The Supreme Court ruled, however, that a federal statute requiring federal firefighters to retire at age 55 does not establish, as a matter of law, that a city's retirement of its firefighters at age 55 is justified under the BFOQ exception to the ADEA. A judge ruling on an ADEA challenge to an age limit errs by giving "any weight, much less conclusive weight, to the federal statute," Justice Marshall stated for a unanimous court. (*Johnson v. Mayor and City Council of Baltimore*)

"Factors Other Than Age" Exception

Like the BFOQ exception, an exception for "reasonable factors other than age" also is narrowly construed. Here are some of the factors that may be considered a valid basis for discrimination under this exception, according to the previous interpretations of the Wage-Hour Administrator:

- Physical fitness requirement based on pre-employment or periodic physical examinations related to standards reasonably necessary for the specific job and uniformly required. But it cannot be assumed that every employee over a certain age automatically becomes unable to meet these physical requirements

- Employee tests that are specifically related to the requirements of the job—with the understanding that older workers generally are not as "test-sophisticated" as younger workers
- Evaluation factors such as quantity or quality of production, or educational level, where the factors have a valid relationship to job requirements and are uniformly applied

Seniority Systems

Employers and unions may observe the terms of a bona fide seniority system "which is not a subterfuge to evade the purposes of the Act." Such a system must make length of service the primary criterion for allocating work opportunities and prerogatives. A reverse seniority system—giving greater rights to junior workers—might be interpreted as a "subterfuge" to evade purposes of the Act, the EEOC states in its interpretations.

Employee Benefit Plans

Under Labor Department rules, an employer is not required to provide older workers with the same pension or insurance benefits provided to younger workers, as long as any differential between them is in accordance with the terms of a bona fide benefit plan. An employer also may provide lesser amounts of insurance coverage to older workers than to younger workers, under a group insurance plan, where the plan is not a subterfuge to evade the Act's purposes.

A retirement or insurance plan is considered nondiscriminatory where the actual amount of payment made or the cost incurred on behalf of an older worker is equal to that made or incurred on behalf of a younger worker, even though the older worker may receive a lesser benefit as a result.

In addition, there is nothing inconsistent with the ADEA in offering older employees compensation for leaving the work force. (*Cipriano v. Board of Education, North Tonawanda*)

1978 Exemptions

The 1986 amendments exempt tenured faculty and state and local public safety officers (police, firefighters, and prison guards) from the mandatory retirement ban for seven years.

ELEMENTS OF AGE DISCRIMINATION CASE

The elements of a prima facie case of illegal age discrimination are analogous to those of a case of Title VII discrimination. The plaintiff must first prove that he or she is a member of the protected age group (age 40 or older) and was adversely affected by the action of an employer, union, or employment agency. Adverse effect may be shown by pointing to a direct act against the employment status of the protected employee, to an act with a differential impact on protected employees, or to a statistical disparity between the percentage of workers 40 or more years old in the employer's work force and the percentage in the relevant labor market.

A prima facie case can be established even if the discharged employee is replaced by an individual within the protected age group. (*Maxfield v. Sinclair International*)

Court Rulings

Judicial decisions involving interpretations of ADEA are being issued in greater numbers by federal courts. Here are some examples:

- The ADEA's defenses based on a "factor other than age" and on a "bona fide employee benefit plan" were not available to an employer, which, on closing its plant, refused to make payments under its LIB (layoff income benefits) plan to employees who were more than 55 years old and thus were eligible for early retirement, an appeals court ruled. (*EEOC v. Westinghouse Electric Corp.*)
- An employer unlawfully denied severance pay to those employees at its closed-down facility who were eligible for retirement, since this amounted to denying them a

benefit because they were age 55 or older. The court found it immaterial that the retirees would receive insurance coverage and pension income that could be worth considerably more than severance pay. (*EEOC v. Borden's Inc.*) However, as a condition of receiving severance pay under a voluntary reduction-in-force program, pension-eligible employees could be required to defer receiving their pension benefits. (*Britt v. E.I. du Pont de Nemours & Co.*)

- Another appeals court ruled that forced early retirement based on economic necessity is unacceptable under the ADEA unless the necessity for drastic cost reduction is shown to be real and forced early retirement is the least-detrimental alternative means available to reduce costs. (*EEOC v. Chrysler Corp.*)

- An employer was found not to have violated the ADEA when, as part of a reduction in the work force, it terminated six employees in the protected age group. The federal district court said that the dismissal was based on factors other than age, since the terminees were selected after evaluation of their ability based on established criteria ordinarily used in the evaluation process. (*Stringfellow v. Monsanto Co.*)

- A desire to establish a new management philosophy by assembling a new management team that displaces older employees does not by itself constitute ADEA discrimination. (*Dale v. Chicago Tribune Co.*)

8
OTHER APPLICATIONS OF EEO LAW

Various additional EEO requirements apply to employers who are federal contractors or subcontractors under several laws and executive orders. Special EEO requirements in regard to handicapped persons apply to programs receiving federal financial assistance and others apply to employers in general. In addition, special applications of EEO laws are in effect for employment agencies, labor unions, and the federal government in its capacity as an employer. All of these topics are discussed below.

FEDERAL CONTRACTORS

Companies doing business with the federal government have an obligation to refrain from employment discrimination that goes beyond that imposed by Title VII. Along with the nondiscrimination requirements of Title VII, government contractors are covered by several executive orders and statutes—administered by the Department of Labor—that bar discrimination on the basis of race, color, religion, sex, national origin, age, handicap, or veteran status, and that require contractors to take affirmative action to ensure equal employment opportunity. There is no prohibition against "preferential" or "quota" hiring. Requirements are as follows:

Executive Orders

Executive Order 11246, as amended (401 FEP Manual 601), covers discrimination based on race, color, religion, sex, or national origin. Executive Order 11141 (401 FEP Manual 615) covers discrimination based on age. Under these orders, government contractors whose amount of business with the government exceeds $10,000 a year must comply with the nondiscrimination requirements. More significantly, however, all contractors with 50 or more employees and contracts of $50,000 or more a year are required to develop written affirmative action plans and to take positive steps to eliminate discrimination within their organizations.

A contractor covered by Executive Order 11246 must

- Refrain from discriminating against any employee or job applicant because of race, color, religion, sex, or national origin
- Take affirmative action to ensure that applicants are employed and employees are treated without regard to race, color, religion, sex, or national origin. (The obligation extends to working conditions and facilities, such as restrooms, as well as to hiring, firing, layoff and recall, promotions, and compensation.)
- State in all advertisements or help solicitations that all qualified applicants will receive consideration without regard to race, color, religion, sex, or national origin
- Advise each labor union with which the contractor deals of its commitments under the Order
- Include the obligation under the Order in every subcontract or purchase order unless specifically exempted
- Comply with all provisions of the Order and the rules and regulations, furnish all information and reports required, and permit access to books, records, and accounts for the purpose of investigation to ascertain compliance
- File regular compliance reports describing hiring and employment practices

Veterans' Readjustment Act

The Vietnam Era Veterans' Readjustment Assistance Act of 1974, as amended (401 FEP Manual 521), requires employers with government contracts or subcontracts of $10,000 or more to take affirmative action "to employ and advance in employment" disabled veterans and qualified veterans of the Vietnam Era. In addition to the affirmative action requirement, the Act imposes an obligation on all covered employers to list all suitable job openings with the appropriate local employment service. Referral priority then will be given to Vietnam Era veterans.

Rehabilitation Act

Section 503 of the Vocational Rehabilitation Act of 1973, as amended (401 FEP Manual 501), requires contractors to take affirmative action and make reasonable accommodations in hiring qualified physically and mentally handicapped persons. The provisions of the Act mandating affirmative action toward the handicapped apply to all federal contractors with contracts of more than $2,500. In addition, under the Labor Department's Affirmative Action Regulations on Handicapped Workers (401 FEP Manual 3021), if the contract is $50,000 or more and the company has 50 or more employees, the contractor must prepare a written affirmative action program and make it available to all employees.

Discrimination against handicapped persons is a relatively new area of concern in EEO law. In many ways, the law against discrimination on the basis of handicap as embodied in Section 503 discussed here and in Section 504 discussed below is similar to the law against discrimination on the basis of race, sex, and national origin—but there are significant differences. There are no numerical hiring goals to achieve, for example. But although there is no need to hire unqualified employees, the concept of affirmative action in Section 503 does require that an employer take steps to accommodate a handicapped worker unless such accommodation poses an undue hardship on the company.

Court opinions vary as to whether handicapped persons have the right to bring private court suits under Section 503 of the Rehabilitation Act. To date, seven federal appeals courts have held that there is no such right.

Affirmative Action Requirements—A company with a government contract exceeding $2,500 must include an affirmative action clause in each of its covered contracts and must post "in conspicuous places" a notice of its affirmative action obligations, as a government contractor, to hire the handicapped. The contractor must also notify every labor union with which it bargains of the contractor's obligations under the Rehabilitation Act.

Companies with contracts of more than $50,000 are required to prepare a written affirmative action program covering the handicapped within 120 days after being granted the contract. The program must be prepared at each of the employer's establishments and may be integrated into its other affirmative action programs. Although there is no obligation to submit the affirmative action plan to the government, it must be available for inspection to any employee or applicant on request. In addition, the programs must be reviewed and updated annually.

Goals and quotas are not required of employers in hiring the handicapped under Section 503. Labor Department regulations emphasize recruitment of the handicapped and communication of the company policy (both within the company and outside it), rather than extensive physical changes.

Employers, however, are obligated to make "reasonable accommodations" to the physical and mental limitations of an employee or applicant unless the contractor can demonstrate that such an accommodation would impose an undue hardship on the conduct of the contractor's business. Such factors as "business necessity" and "financial cost and expenses" will be taken into account.

Some of the major provisions required under the Labor Department regulations regarding affirmative action programs and the handicapped are as follows:

- In making recruitment efforts, the Labor Department notes, the scope "shall depend upon all the circumstances, including the contractor's size and resources and the extent to which existing employment practices are adequate." State vocational rehabilitation agencies, sheltered workshops, schools for the handicapped, and social service agencies are suggested as sources for recruitment efforts.

- Contractors are to provide in their affirmative action programs a schedule for review of all physical or mental job qualification requirements to ensure that, to the extent that they screen out qualified handicapped individuals, they are job-related and consistent with business necessity and the safe performance of the job.

• Companies still may conduct physical examinations of job applicants so long as they are not used to exclude qualified handicapped individuals. Any inquiries as to an applicant's or employee's physical or mental conditions are to be kept confidential except that: (1) supervisors may be informed regarding work restrictions and accommodations that may be necessary; (2) first aid and medical personnel may be informed if the condition might require emergency treatment; and (3) government officials investigating compliance must be informed.

While American citizens working overseas in businesses with covered federal contracts are protected by the Vocational Rehabilitation Act, foreigners working in the same businesses are not. Whether employees of conglomerates are covered depends on the exact nature of the corporate arrangement and the nature of the government contract.

A waiver of the affirmative action obligation may be granted by the head of a contracting agency to an otherwise covered employer where the waiver is deemed to be in the "national interest," or in the "interest of national security." The Secretary of Labor must concur in the waiver, where the contention is "national interest," but this concurrence is not required where the claim is "national security." The waiver procedure is hardly ever used.

The affirmative action requirements also may be waived at any of the contractor's facilities found to be "in all respects separate and distinct" from the facilities involved in performance of the government contract. The waiver will be considered, however, only if requested by the contractor or subcontractor.

Additional information on requirements under the Rehabilitation Act, including definitions of persons considered handicapped, as well as information on other laws applied in this area of EEO concern, appears below.

HANDICAP DISCRIMINATION PROHIBITIONS

In addition to the Section 503 affirmative action requirements for federal contractors discussed above, the Vocational Rehabilitation Act under Section 504 prohibits discrimination against handicapped persons in programs or activities receiving federal financial assistance. The Supreme Court has ruled that an action to enforce Section 504 can be brought among recipients even though the federal aid received is not for the "primary purpose" of "promoting employment." (*Consolidated Rail Corp. v. Darrone*)

A discussion of definitions in the Act which apply to both Sections 503 and 504 follows.

Definition of Handicapped Person

For purposes of both Sections 503 and 504 of the Rehabilitation Act a handicapped individual is a person "who has a physical or mental impairment which substantially limits one or more of such person's major life activities." Such a limitation is evidenced if the individual is likely to experience difficulty in securing, retaining, or advancing in employment because of a handicap, according to the Labor Department's Affirmative Action Regulations on Handicapped Workers (401 FEP Manual 3021) relating to Section 503 and to the Department's Rules on Handicap Discrimination in Federally Assisted Programs (401 FEP Manual 541) covering Section 504.

However, the Act also considers as handicapped those individuals who have a record of such an impairment or are "regarded as having" an impairment. Individuals who may be completely recovered from a previous physical or mental impairment (such as the mentally restored, or those who have had heart attacks or cancer), for example, often have difficulty in job situations because of their handicap histories, and, as such, receive protection under the Act.

The Act also protects individuals who may have been erroneously classified as handicapped (such as the mentally retarded) and may have experienced discrimination based on this miscalculation. In addition, the Labor Department has taken the position that alcoholics and drug abusers are within the protection of the Vocational Rehabilitation Act; it was the intention of Congress to cover these two groups, the Department has said. It has emphasized, however, that an employer must hire and promote only "qualified handicapped workers."

A newly employed worker who was discharged by the U.S. Postal Service after her bad back prevented her from performing all duties of her job was not an "otherwise qualified handicapped person" under Section 504 of the Act because she was not "otherwise qualified" for her job, an appeals court ruled. (*Daubert v. United States Postal Service*)

Other Applicable Laws

The majority of states now include the handicapped within the provisions of their FEP laws, thus extending requirements to employers beyond the group affected by similar rules under Sections 503 and 504 of the Vocational Rehabilitation Act.

In deciding cases involving discrimination against handicapped workers, the courts have tended to rely either on constitutional guarantees or on these state laws rather than on the Rehabilitation Act. Some examples of court decisions are as follows:

- A newly hired employee was found to have been terminated unlawfully under the Wisconsin State Fair Employment Act because he had a history of asthma. The court said the termination violated the Act because the employee was in the protected group of handicapped in that, although his disease made achievement difficult, he still was capable of performing the work efficiently. (*Milwaukee Road v. Wisconsin DILHR*)

- A Pennsylvania school district violated the due process clause of the Constitution by refusing to consider a blind applicant for a position as a secondary school English teacher. The summary rejection of the application, the court said, created a presumption that blind persons cannot be competent teachers for students with sight. (*Gurmankin v. Costanzo*)

- Employers are obligated not to reject a prospective employee because of a physical or mental handicap unless as a result of the defect there is "a probability either that the employee cannot do the job in a satisfactory manner or that he can do so only at the risk of incapacitating himself," the Oregon Supreme Court ruled, interpreting the state civil rights act. (*Montgomery Ward v. Bureau of Labor*)

- The term "visually handicapped" includes persons with eye impairments less serious than total or functional blindness, a North Carolina Court of Appeals held, reinstating an employment bias suit filed by a job applicant suffering from glaucoma, which was controlled through medication. (*Burgess v. Joseph Schlitz Brewing Co.*)

- An employer's refusal to hire a qualified handicapped individual because of a prospective physical disability is prohibited by the California Fair Employment and Housing Act, the California Court of Appeals decided. (*Sterling Transit Co., Inc. v. FEPC*)

- California could not be sued under the Rehabilitation Act of 1973 for allegedly denying employment to a job applicant because he was diabetic and blind in one eye, the Supreme Court ruled. The Court held that the suit was barred by the Eleventh Amendment, and it decided that California's acceptance of funds under the Act and its participation in programs funded under that statute did not waive its constitutional immunity to suit. (*Atascadero State Hospital v. Scanlon*)

- An appeals court ruled that a police officer who was discharged for use of heroin is not a "handicapped individual" under Section 504, where his drug habit rendered him unfit for police work. (*Heron v. McGuire*)

AIDS AND OTHER CONTAGIOUS DISEASES

Many states are accepting AIDS-related discrimination complaints under their laws prohibiting handicap discrimination.

The Supreme Court may ultimately determine whether a person with AIDS is "handicapped" under the Rehabilitation

Act of 1973. One appeals court ruled that a chronic contagious disease, such as tuberculosis, is a "handicap" within the meaning of Section 504 of the Act. (*Arline v. Nassau County School Board*)

FEDERAL FINANCIAL ASSISTANCE RECIPIENTS

Title VI of the Civil Rights Act of 1964 bars discrimination by recipients of federal financial assistance, such as school districts and police departments.

Sex discrimination is not specifically prohibited by Title VI, but some federal agencies have barred such bias in their regulations.

A showing of discriminatory intent is necessary to establish a violation of Title VI, the Supreme Court has ruled. (*Guardians Association v. Civil Service Commission*)

EMPLOYMENT AGENCIES

Employment agencies often have a key position in the hiring process. For this reason, they are given specific attention in Title VII as well as in other federal and state laws and orders regulating employment discrimination.

Under Title VII, it is an unlawful employment practice for an employment agency

- To fail or refuse to refer for employment or otherwise to discriminate against any person because of his or her race, color, religion, sex, or national origin
- To classify or refer any person for employment on the basis of his or her race, color, religion, sex, or national origin

These prohibitions apply not only to private employment agencies, but also to the United States Employment Service and state and local employment services that receive federal assistance.

Employment agencies servicing covered employers also are included under the provisions of the Age Discrimination in Employment Act of 1967, as amended (401 FEP Manual 351), and are thus prohibited from refusing to refer individuals for employment because of age and from classifying or referring for employment on the basis of age.

LABOR UNIONS

The obligations imposed on labor organizations by Title VII have two aspects. First, where a union acts as an employer, it has the same duty as any other employer not to discriminate in employment on the basis of race, color, religion, sex, national origin, or age.

Second, in its capacity as a union, it may not

- Exclude, expel from membership, or otherwise discriminate against a person because of his or her race, color, religion, sex, national origin, or age
- Limit, segregate, or classify membership and membership applicants or fail or refuse to refer an individual for employment in any way that would deprive or tend to deprive that individual of employment opportunities or would limit such employment opportunities or otherwise adversely affect the individual's status as an employee or applicant for employment because of the individual's race, color, religion, sex, national origin, or age
- Cause or attempt to cause an employer to discriminate against an individual because of his or her race, color, religion, sex, national origin, or age
- Operate or join with employers in the operation of an apprenticeship training or retraining program in which discrimination on the basis of race, color, religion, sex, national origin, or age is practiced

Nondiscrimination Clause

Under the policies of the EEOC, a union has a duty not only to refrain from engaging in discriminatory practices of its own but also of challenging discriminatory practices of employers with whom the union bargains. This becomes particularly important where there is no nondiscrimination clause in the collective bargaining contract or where the contract has a seniority clause found to have a discriminatory effect. In such a case, the union and the employer may be held jointly liable for back pay to the employees against whom there was unlawful discrimination. Examples of decisions in this area include the following:

- If a union has a nondiscrimination clause in its contract, its failure to use it to protest discriminatory practices of the employer may be considered a violation of Title VII by the EEOC. (EEOC Decision No. 71-27)
- Moreover, a union's failure to propose a nondiscrimination clause in its contract may be considered a violation by the EEOC. In one case, a failure to process grievances of black members who alleged discrimination was considered not to be justified by the absence of a nondiscrimination clause in the union's contract. (EEOC Decision No. 71-90)
- Along the same lines, a union's failure to propose an alternative to a seniority system that perpetuated the effects of past unlawful discrimination was considered by the EEOC to be a violation of Title VII (EEOC Decision No. 71-484), as was a refusal to publish the collective bargaining agreement in Spanish where a substantial number of the employees spoke and read only Spanish. (EEOC Decision No. 71-2029) See Chapter 11 for a further discussion of EEO requirements applicable to seniority systems.

Admission Standards

As a general rule, the courts have held that union admission standards that operate in a manner that unnecessarily disqualifies individuals for membership on the basis of color, sex, national origin, or age are unlawful. In the early years of enforcement of the 1964 Civil Rights Act, courts made these rulings:

- A local union was found to have engaged in a "pattern or practice" of discrimination against blacks and Mexican-Americans by maintaining membership rules that required that a new member be related to a present member, recommended by a member of the local, and approved by a majority vote. The local was ordered to suspend the membership standards, admit four complainants, and refer nine others for immediate employment. (*Vogler v. McCarty, Inc.*)

- Two local unions were found to be carrying on the effects of past discrimination with respect to apprenticeship, membership, and job referral, despite the fact that their policy had changed to include blacks after the adoption of Title VII. The unions were ordered to modify the experience requirement for blacks, as well as the journeyman's examination, and to give those blacks beyond the apprenticeship age the opportunity to take the journeyman's test. (*United States v. Sheet Metal Workers, Local 36*)

Union Referral Systems

A union which formerly operated a hiring hall on a discriminatory basis and then established a referral system giving credit for experience gained under the old system is regarded by the courts as having violated Title VII. A union with a disproportionately low number of women as members also was found to have violated Title VII when it made and enforced a collective bargaining contract requiring studios in the stage and motion picture industry to give preference to union members on an industry experience roster. Because the roster rarely was exhausted, women were unable to gain the experience necessary for membership in the union and placement on the roster. (*Kaplan v. Stage Employees, Local 659*)

However, neither contractor associations that negotiate labor agreements nor employers that use the exclusive hiring hall established by those agreements are vicariously liable for a union's racially discriminatory operation of a hiring hall. (*General Building Contractors Association v. Pennsylvania*)

Fair Representation

Under the Taft-Hartley Act, the Railway Labor Act, and Title VII, a union that is an exclusive bargaining representative has an obligation to represent all members of the bargaining unit fairly and on a nondiscriminatory basis. In the leading case of *Vaca v. Sipes*, the Supreme Court held that if a union's actions are "arbitrary, discriminatory, or in bad faith," they may amount to unfair representation. Moreover, negligence of a union in processing a grievance may provide a basis for a finding of a breach of fair representation.

The Supreme Court added to this doctrine in a later case involving the discharge of a group of employees for dishonesty. The union carried the case through the grievance arbitration procedure under the contract, and the arbitrator denied the grievance. Later, evidence was discovered that showed that the charges against the grievants were not true. But the union did no more, and lower courts refused to upset the arbitration decision, stating that the contract contained a provision that an arbitration award would be "final and binding," and it would impair the arbitration process to permit the issue to be relitigated.

The Supreme Court disagreed. Where the contractual processes have been flawed by the union's failure to represent employees honestly, in good faith, and without invidious discrimination or arbitrary conduct, the Court said, the employees may sue on their own with their own counsel under Section 301 of the Taft-Hartley Act. (*Hines v. Anchor Motor Freight, Inc.*)

Bypassing Union

If a group of minority employees do not first exhaust their contractual remedies and instead bypass their collective bargaining representative and act on their own to eliminate discrimination, they may lose their protection under the Taft-Hartley Act.

In a case involving a San Francisco department store, two black employees picketed the store and distributed handbills to protest the alleged racial discrimination by the employer. They were discharged. At the time the employees picketed, the union representing them was pursuing a grievance involving the alleged racial discrimination. The Supreme Court held that by acting in derogation of their collective bargaining representative the employees lost their protection under the Taft-Hartley Act, and so the employer lawfully could discharge them. (*Emporium Capwell Co. v. WACO*)

Remedies for Union Discrimination

The courts have prescribed a variety of remedies, including affirmative action, in cases in which they have found unions have engaged in or caused discrimination.

In one case, for example, a construction union was found to have engaged in discrimination by failing to admit nonwhites to full journeyman status, discriminating against them in work referral, and participating in a discriminatory apprenticeship program. The Second Circuit ordered the union to adopt an affirmative action program to bring nonwhite participation in the union to a set percentage. The court said that the program was not barred by the preference or quota provision of Title VII; that provision, it added, prohibits only quota hiring used to remedy racial imbalance not caused by unlawful discrimination. (*Rios v. Steamfitters, Local 638*)

Other Obligations

Unions, as well as employers, have a responsibility to see that the equal pay laws are carried our for their membership, particularly when they are at the bargaining table. A collective bargaining contract perpetuating prior pay discrimination affords an employer no defense to the charge of violating the Equal Pay Act of 1963 (401 FEP Manual 451), and if the union also contributed to the discriminatory scheme, a claimant has a cause of action against the union as well. (*Laffey v. Northwest Airlines*)

Labor unions with 25 or more members also are included under the provisions of the Age Discrimination in Employment Act of 1967 and are forbidden from excluding or expelling individuals from membership on the basis of age.

FEDERAL GOVERNMENT AS EMPLOYER

The protection expressly granted employees of private employers by Title VII was extended to federal employees by the 1972 amendments to the Civil Rights Act of 1964. A provision of those amendments spells out the obligations of the federal government to ensure that all personnel actions affecting employees or applicants for jobs in the federal service be free from discrimination based on race, color, religion, sex, or national origin.

Title VII is not the only EEO statute applying to federal employees. A series of executive orders and various laws, most discussed earlier in this book, also prohibit job discrimination or promote equal employment opportunity in the federal sector:

- Executive Order 11478 (401 FEP Manual 1101) prohibits discrimination on the basis of race, color, religion, sex, and national origin.
- Executive Order 11141 (401 FEP Manual 615) prohibits discrimination on the basis of age.
- Executive Order 11935 (401 FEP Manual 1105) prohibits the employment of aliens in the U.S. competitive civil service.
- Executive Order 12125 (401 FEP Manual 1105) exempts "severely" physically handicapped and mentally retarded individuals from competitive examinations for federal government jobs.
- Under 1974 amendments to the Fair Labor Standards Act, protection under both the Age Discrimination in Employment Act (401 FEP Manual 351) and the Equal Pay Act (401 FEP Manual 451) was extended to federal employees. While the 1978 amendments to the ADEA raised the permissible mandatory retirement age for most private sector employees from 65 to 70, for federal workers the amendments removed the upper age limit of 70, effective September 30, 1978. Despite this, the Supreme Court has held that, even though other federal workers no longer are subject to a mandatory retirement age, a mandatory retirement age of 60 for Foreign Service employees does not violate the constitutional guarantee of equal protection. (*Vance v. Bradley*)
- Both the Vocational Rehabilitation Act (401 FEP Manual 501), applying to handicapped workers, and the Vietnam Era Veterans' Readjustment Act (401 FEP Manual 521), impose special obligations on federal government agencies to take affirmative action in providing jobs for the

handicapped, disabled veterans, and veterans of the Vietnam War.

Court Decisions

Judicial decisions in the area of EEO law covering federal employees include the following:

- A postal employee is not required to submit direct evidence of discriminatory intent in order to prevail in his claim. (*Aikens v. United States Postal Service Board of Governors*)
- Although an individual complainant is required to exhaust administrative remedies before bringing suit, this restriction does not apply where class actions are involved, a court of appeals ruled. When a federal employee brings a class action on behalf of other federal employees, the court said, those employees are not required to demonstrate as well that each has exhausted available administrative remedies. (*Williams v. TVA*)
- Title VII is the exclusive judicial remedy for discrimination suits filed by federal employees, the Supreme Court has ruled, despite contentions by civil rights groups that federal employees should be able to bring suits under other statutes. The 1972 Civil Rights Act amendments indicated that Congress intended to create "an exclusive pre-emptive administrative and judicial scheme for the redress of federal employment discrimination," the Court said. (*Brown v. GSA*)
- Once an employee or job applicant has taken a claim to court, the court is not bound by the findings or conclusion of the federal agency involved. The legislative history of the 1972 amendments indicated that the "civil action" to which federal employees are entitled is a trial de novo, not just a review of the administrative record of their discrimination claim, according to the Supreme Court. (*Chandler v. Roudebush*)
- In *Vergara v. Chairman, Merit Systems Protection Board*, the Supreme Court refused to review a lower court decision which upheld Executive Order 11935 barring resident aliens from federal civil service positions. Earlier, before

the order was issued, in *Hampton v. Wong* the Court had said that the Civil Service exceeded its authority by banning aliens from federal jobs pursuant to its own regulations. The Court noted, however, that if the president has "expressly imposed the citizenship requirement," it would be justified. As a result, President Ford issued the executive order three months later imposing the citizenship requirements, and the order was subsequently upheld in *Vergara*.

- Title VII's prohibitions against retaliation and harassment apply to federal employees, as well as those in the private sector, a court of appeals ruled. (*Ayon v. Sampson*)
- When Congress extended Title VII to include federal government employees, it did not intend to cover persons who enlist or apply for enlistment in any of the armed forces, according to a court of appeals. Military service differs from ordinary employment since an enlisted soldier is not free to quit his or her "job" nor can the Army fire the individual, the court pointed out. If Congress had intended to apply Title VII to the uniformed military, it would have said so "in unmistakable terms," the court concluded. (*Johnson v. Alexander*)
- Declaring that the United States does not have an "infinite ability to pay," another court of appeals suggested that fees in employment discrimination cases against the federal government should reflect the lawyer's cost plus a reasonable profit for the firm, rather than a standard cost per hour. (*Copeland v. Marshall*)
- The Federal Bureau of Investigation violated a homosexual employee's due process rights by terminating him without a hearing, the U.S. Court of Appeals for the District of Columbia held. (*Ashton V. Civiletti*)
- A newly employed worker who was discharged by the U.S. Postal Service after her bad back prevented her from performing all the duties of her job was not an "otherwise qualified person" under Section 504 of the Rehabilitation Act of 1973, since she was not "otherwise qualified" for her job. (*Daubert v. United States Postal Service*)

- Although the U.S. Department of Agriculture's print shop was racially integrated, it did not insulate the department from liability for intentional discrimination against an individual employee. (*Bibbs v. Block*)

PART 3

POLICY AND PRACTICE ISSUES

9
RECRUITING, HIRING, AND PROMOTION

There are certain issues in EEO law that concern several forbidden types of discrimination. Among those issues are recruiting, hiring, and promoting; employment testing; employment conditions; seniority and layoffs; retaliation; and reverse discrimination. Each is discussed in this Part.

An essential ingredient to a nondiscriminatory employment policy under the federal laws and executive orders is a basic procedure for recruiting and selecting new employees that does not intentionally or inadvertently work to screen out minority group members, women, or other protected groups. A company also must be able to show that it uses nondiscriminatory standards in selecting employees for promotion. Typically, the selection process is often the first place that federal officials will look in judging whether a company is in compliance with EEO law.

RECRUITING AND HIRING

An employer is not required to go out and hire a designated quota of members of minorities and other protected groups. But a serious imbalance in the number of such workers in the work force when compared to the proportion in the area, may suggest to federal officials that something is wrong with hiring policies. Reliance on walk-in applicants and "word-of-mouth" recruiting, for example, may not be regarded as enough if the work force is predominantly white. Furthermore, hiring stand-

89

ards may be suspect if they are not job-related, but rather reflect the norms of the white community.

Determinations by the courts and the EEOC as to whether particular recruiting or promoting policies are discriminatory usually are based on the test laid down by the Supreme Court in *Griggs v. Duke Power Co.* In that landmark case, the Court decreed that if an action or policy, although neutral on its face, is discriminatory in effect, it is unlawful unless it is shown there is a substantial business justification for the policy. Furthermore, an appeals court ruled, pretext is not irrelevant in a disparate impact case, since a plaintiff may prevail by proving that an employer's hiring practices, for example, are pretext for discrimination—even if the employer demonstrates a business necessity for the practices. *(Kilgo v. Bowman Transportation)* A more detailed discussion of requirements regarding selection practices appears in the next chapter.

Applying the *Griggs* test, the courts and the EEOC have found unlawful recruiting and hiring policies in the following situations:

- A company's refusal to hire job applicants because of their arrest record. *(Gregory v. Litton Systems, Inc.; Green v. Missouri Pacific R.R.)* But such a refusal to hire was held justified where it involved a hotel bellman who would have access to guests' luggage and rooms. *(Richardson v. Hotel Corp. of America)*
- Word-of-mouth recruiting or recruiting at only predominantly white educational institutions where there is an existing racial imbalance in the work force *(United States v. Georgia Power;* EEOC Decision No. 72-0599)
- A requirement that applicants have a high school education where there is no showing that the requirement is sufficiently related to job performance to be warranted *(United States v. Georgia Power Co.)*
- Recruiting personnel for a television station from employees of radio stations under the same ownership, where evidence clearly showed that the hiring policies of the radio stations discriminated against women *(EEOC v. New York Times Broadcasting Service)*

- Refusal to employ individuals fined for gambling (EEOC Decision No. 71-2682)
- Refusal to employ individuals because of their poor credit record (EEOC Decision No. 72-0427)
- Rejection of applicants based on adverse personnel reports from other companies without giving applicants an opportunity to rebut the report (EEOC Decision Nos. 72-0947, 72-2103)
- Preferential hiring of relatives of present employees where the present work force contains a disproportionately low percentage of minority workers (EEOC Decision No. 71-797)
- A requirement for union membership and listing on an experience roster for job referrals which has the effect of excluding a greater proportion of women than men from available jobs (*Kaplan v. Stage Employees, Local 659*)
- Use of a minimum height requirement where it had the effect of excluding a substantially greater number of women and Spanish-surnamed Americans than Caucasian males (EEOC Decision No. 71-1418; *Dothard v. Rawlinson; Davis v. County of Los Angeles*)
- Denial of employment to unwed mothers in an area where blacks had a significantly higher rate of illegitimate births and where there was no showing of business necessity (EEOC Decision No. 71-332)

Prior Hiring Practices

The extent to which an employer's past hiring practices have resulted in a predominantly white work force may well determine the extent to which the federal agencies will require affirmative acts to recruit from minority group sources. Both the EEOC and the OFCCP have taken the position that an employer with a disproportionately low number of minority group members in its work force probably has acquired a reputation as being discriminatory. In such a case, the mere announcement of a policy of equal employment opportunity may not be regarded as enough to offset the past reputation. Reliance on "word-of-mouth" recruiting, for example, by an employer with a predominantly white work force will only perpetuate the existing racial make-up of the work force, in the view of federal officials. Once a good racial mix is achieved in the work force, however, an employer presumably could rely on walk-in applicants and word-of-mouth recruiting.

An employer whose past hiring practices have resulted in a good minority group representation among production workers is not necessarily in the clear either, however. A disproportionately low number of minority group members in white-collar, professional, or supervisory jobs may suggest to enforcement agencies that special recruiting efforts are needed in these areas. Where an employer traditionally has excluded blacks as a class from certain jobs, such as management or clerical, the employer is required under Title VII to communicate effectively to the black community the face that it has abandoned its discriminatory policies and practices. *(United States v. Sheet Metal Workers, Local 36)*

Pre-Employment Inquiries

Pre-employment inquiries concerning race, color, religion, or national origin are not, by themselves, a violation of Title VII. But the EEOC regards such inquiries as totally irrelevant to an applicant's ability or qualification, except in those rare instances where religion or national origin is a bona fide occupational qualification. Hence, such inquiries, unless otherwise explained, may be regarded as evidence of such discrimination. (EEOC Decision, 12/30/65) Examples of other EEOC decisions in this regard include the following:

- A pre-employment inquiry made pursuant to the requirements of a local, state, or federal FEP law will not constitute evidence of discrimination. (EEOC Opinion, 5/27/68)
- A requirement that a photograph accompany an employment application may be regarded as evidence of discrimination. (EEOC Decision, 1/4/66)
- Coding of employment applications by case for the purpose of complying with the affirmative action requirements of a government contract is not a violation of the

1964 Civil Rights Act, the EEOC has indicated. Subsequent coding of employment applications, however, would be in violation of the law if it were done for the purpose of, or had the effect of, illegally discriminating among applicants of different races. (Letter from Associate Solicitor of Labor, February 7, 1972)

Post-Employment Inquiries

The EEOC recognizes that inquiries as to an employee's race, sex, or national origin sometimes are useful or even necessary for reporting purposes or to permit an employer to evaluate its personnel program. In such cases, the EEOC strongly recommends that the requested information be kept completely separate from the files of individual employees. If feasible, such data should be maintained simply as a running total rather than as a record of individual employees' status. (EEOC General Counsel Opinion Letter, 10/12/66)

Hiring Standards

Affirmative recruiting efforts that substantially increase the flow of minority group applicants will not satisfy the EEOC or the OFCCP if, due to unreasonably high standards for hire, few of these applicants are hired.

Both the EEOC and the OFCCP will be on the lookout for hiring standards that are not job-related, but rather reflect the norms of the white community. Employers must be prepared to demonstrate that their hiring standards do not automatically screen out applicants whose speech, dress, and personal work habits differ from those of the predominant groups. Rejection of a job applicant because of his or her appearance and manner of speaking may be regarded as unlawful if the appearance and manner of speaking are peculiar to the applicant's race or national origin. (EEOC Decision No. AL68-1-155E)

Examples of decisions in this area include the following:

- The Supreme Court held lawful the New York City Transit Authority's policy of denying employment to all current methadone users. The policy had been challenged on the ground that it had a discriminatory effect on blacks and Hispanics in violation of Title VII and the equal protection clause of the 14th Amendment. *(New York City Transit Authority v. Beazer)*

● It is unlawful to discharge or to refuse to employ a minority group person because of a conviction record unless the particular circumstances of each case indicate that employment of that particular person for a particular job is manifestly inconsistent with the safe and efficient operation of that job, the EEOC has held. (EEOC Decision No. 72-1460) Thus, an automatic disqualification of any job applicant who has a police record might be viewed as arbitrary by the EEOC or the OFCCP. More appropriate would be a case-by-case approach which takes into consideration the number and types of charges, whether they resulted in convictions, how long ago arrests occurred, the applicant's age at the time of arrest, and his or her subsequent behavior.

● Similarly suspect are educational requirements that are not job-related. The U.S. Supreme Court has ruled that a company that uses employment tests or other job screening standards, such as possession of a high school diploma, must be able to show that they are "demonstrably a reasonable measure of job performance." The Court left open, however, the question of whether an employer may use tests or other screening requirements that take into account capability for future promotions. *(Griggs v. Duke Power)*

● However, the courts have upheld some educational requirements; one court of appeals upheld the educational requirement for Boston policemen, which can be met by graduation from high school, by a certificate of equivalency, or by an honorable discharge after three years of military service. *(Castro v. Beecher)*

Quota Hiring

There is no hiring issue that arouses more fury and passion than the question of the use of quotas. Title VII differs substantially from Executive Order 11246 on this issue. An explicit ban on quota hiring (for example, 11 percent of the area population is black, therefore, 11 percent of the hires should be blacks) is contained in Title VII. The language of Title VII, however, has been held not to bar quota hiring used to remedy racial imbalance caused by unlawful discriminatory conduct. Accordingly, once a Title VII violation was established, a district court has imposed a hiring quota as a remedy. (*Rios v. Steamfitters, Local 638*)

However, in a major ruling, the Supreme Court held that Title VII does not permit the affirmative action goals of a consent decree benefiting employees who were not "actual victims" of discrimination to be given greater protection than a bona fide seniority system in the event of unanticipated layoffs. (*Firefighters, Local 1784 v. Stotts*)

The Court found support for its position in the legislative history to Title VII. In its opinion, the Court italicized a portion of an interpretive memorandum by the bill's Republican House sponsors: *"Title VII does not permit the ordering of racial quotas in business or unions."*

Unlike Title VII, however, Executive Order 11246 does not contain an explicit ban on quota hiring. Instead, it requires contractors to "take affirmative action to ensure the applicants are employed without regard to their race, color, religion, sex, or national origin."

In 1979, the Supreme Court decided *Steelworkers v. Weber*, a landmark case involving quota hiring under both Title VII and the Executive Order. The case involved a quota system which assigned black employees to a training program over white employees with more seniority. The system was implemented by a company to remedy the disparity between the percentage of blacks in the company's work force. The quota system was implemented voluntarily to avoid "vexatious" litigation by minority employees and to comply with OFCCP regulations.

Rejecting a white worker's claim of reverse discrimination, the Supreme Court endorsed the legality of the affirmative action program, voluntarily implemented by both the employer and union to boost employment opportunities for minorities.

The Court declared that adoption of the plan "falls within the area of discretion left by Title VII to the private sector voluntarily to adopt affirmative action plans designed to eliminate conspicuous racial imbalance in traditionally segregated job categories."

PROMOTIONS

An appeals court ruled that a public employer did not violate Title VII by promoting a female employee pursuant to an affirmative action plan over a more qualified male employee. The agency's affirmative action plan met the *Weber* test, the court stated. In demonstrating that its plan is remedial, the court said that an employer does not have to show that it purposely discriminated in the past. Rather, the appeals court said, it is sufficient for the employer to show a conspicuous imbalance in its work force. (*Johnson v. Transportation Agency, Santa Clara County*)

An employer's policies for selecting employees for promotion generally must meet the same test set forth in *Griggs v. Duke Power Co.* and related decisions regarding policies for recruiting and hiring. Decisions under this standard include the following:

- An appeals court held it unlawful for an employer to rely solely on company foremen to recommend employees for transfer and promotion where it was shown that a disproportionately small percentage of black hourly employees were promoted or transferred to salaried positions and the standards used by the foremen were subjective and without any safeguards to insure impartiality. (*Rowe v. General Motors Corp.*)
- In promotions, as with hirings, the employer has the burden of proving business necessity if it is to be allowed to adhere to a challenged practice. It must be able to show not only a business purpose for the practice but also that the practice could not be replaced by another procedure that would be just as efficacious for the business purpose but have a lesser racial impact. (*Head v. Timken Roller Bearing Co.*)

- A federal district court did not abuse its discretion when it rejected a one-to-one promotion quota provision of a proposed consent decree that would have settled a Title VII action against a police department. *(Williams v. City of New Orleans)*
- While approving an order requiring a police department to have 15 percent of its force composed of blacks and Puerto Ricans, an appeals court refused to go along with imposition of quotas on ranks above that of patrolman. Imposition of promotional quotas obviously would discriminate against whites who embarked on a police career with the expectation of advancement and would "only exacerbate rather than diminish racial attitudes," the court held. *(Bridgeport Guardians, Inc. v. Commission)*
- However, in another case with reverse discrimination implications, the Supreme Court affirmed that a federal district court was not required to allow white troopers to present evidence on the "harsh impact" that the imposition of promotional quotas would have on them when the quota order was consistent with the purposes of Title VII, did not unnecessarily trammel the interests of the white troopers, did not absolutely bar advancement to corporal, and was a temporary measure. *(United States v. Paradise)*
- When blacks have been passed over in the past for promotions, it may be regarded as unlawful to disqualify them from current openings on the ground that they are too old to promote. (EEOC Decision No. YAU 9-144)
- An employee whose race played a "discernible part" in his or her loss of a promotion is entitled to a retroactive promotion plus back pay, unless his or her employer shows that it would not have promoted him or her even absent discrimination. *(Bibbs v. Block)*

THE BUSINESS NECESSITY STANDARD

Although the Supreme Court in *Griggs v. Duke Power Co.* indicated that a policy that had a discriminatory impact might be justified on grounds of business necessity, the EEOC and the courts have given this exception a narrow reading. The Supreme Court in *Griggs* made it clear that business necessity did not encompass such matters as inconvenience, annoyance, or expense to the employer. The only permissible reason for tolerating a policy with discriminatory impact is business necessity that is "related to job performance," the Court said.

Other courts have added these interpretations of business necessity as justification for policies that have a discriminatory effect:

- The test is "not merely whether there exists a business purpose for adhering to a challenged practice." Rather, "the test is whether the alleged purpose is so essential to the safe and efficient operation of the business as to override any racial impact." *(Robinson v. P. Lorillard Co.)*

- "Necessity connotes an irresistible demand." In order to be preserved, the practice "must not only directly foster safety and efficiency" but also "must be essential to those goals.... If the legitimate goals of safety and efficiency can be served by a reasonably available alternative system with less discriminatory effects, then the ... system may not be retained." *(United States v. Bethlehem Steel Co.)*

- The employer's burden of proof in establishing a business necessity may vary depending upon the nature of the job, an appeals court noted in upholding an airline's requirement of a college degree and 500 hours of flight time for the position of flight officer. *(Spurlock v. United Airlines)*

- If a facially neutral job criterion is "manifestly job-related," even if it has an adverse impact upon minority workers an employer does not need to prove business necessity, an appeals court ruled. *(Smith v. Olin Chemical Corp.)*

10

EMPLOYMENT TESTS AND OTHER SELECTION PROCEDURES

One of the most troublesome aspects of EEO enforcement since the passage of Title VII has been the use of tests and other selecting devices. In 1964, the EEOC issued a set of Guidelines on Employment Testing Procedures, but in 1968 the OFCCP issued its own set of selection guidelines for government contractors. It was only after ten years of controversy and negotiation among several government agencies involved in EEO enforcement that the Uniform Guidelines on Employee Selection Procedures (401 FEP Manual 2231) became effective, replacing the two previous conflicting sets of federal guidelines. Announcement of the single set of federal guidelines culminated the effort to set forth procedures that public and private employers must use to prove that their employee selection practices, including testing, are nondiscriminatory.

BASIC PRINCIPLE

The basic principle underlying the Uniform Guidelines is that employer policies or practices—formal testing, as well as any other procedures such as interviews, assessment centers, or any qualification used for selection purposes—that have an adverse impact on employment opportunities of any race, sex, or ethnic group are illegal under Title VII and Executive Order 11246, unless justified by business necessity. An employer generally will not be subject to the Guidelines if its selection testing procedures are not found to have an adverse impact on minorities or women. If an adverse impact is found, an employer can modify or eliminate the testing procedure, or take the alternative route of validation, that is, showing the procedure is job-related. The bulk of the Guidelines consists of the government's interpretation of validation standards based on the recognized types of validity studies. The importance of a careful job analysis is emphasized.

Title VII expressly authorizes the use of "any professionally developed ability test *provided* that such test, its administration or action upon the results is not designed, intended or used to discriminate because of race, color, religion, sex, or national origin."

Prior to the promulgation of the Uniform Guidelines, the Supreme Court ruled in *Griggs v. Duke Power Co.* that any selection criterion which has an adverse effect on women or minority group applicants must be validated as job-related. In the landmark *Griggs* case the Court found that the employer's requirement of a high school diploma and a passing score on a standardized general intelligence test for hiring and promotion purposes violated Title VII because (1) neither was shown to be significantly related to successful job performance, (2) both requirements operate to disqualify blacks at a substantially higher rate than whites, and (3) the jobs in question formerly had been filled only by white employees as part of a long-standing practice of giving preference to whites. Selection procedures are "useful," the Court concluded, but Congress has commanded that "any tests used must measure the person for the job and not the person in the abstract."

On the other hand, the Supreme Court later held in *Washington v. Davis* that the standards for a Title VII challenge and a constitutional challenge are not the same. To be successful, a Title VII challenge must establish only that the test has a discriminatory impact, regardless of the employer's intent, while a successful constitutional equal protection challenge requires proof both of discriminatory impact and of intent, the Court said.

The Uniform Guidelines require employers to maintain detailed records from which a determination can be made as to whether a selection procedure has an adverse impact on a protected group. Where an employer has failed to keep the required documentation, a federal enforcement agency may infer that an adverse impact exists "if the user has an underutilization of a group in the job category."

Adverse Impact

The Uniform Guidelines adopt a "rule of thumb" as a practical means of determining "adverse impact" for use in enforcement proceedings. Known as the four-fifths or "80 percent" rule, it says that a selection rate for any racial, ethnic, or sex group which is less than four-fifths of the rate for the group with the highest rate will generally be regarded by the federal enforcement agencies as evidence of adverse impact.

COURT CHALLENGES

Court challenges to testing and other selection devices follow the general order and allocation of proof for disparate (adverse) impact cases. The challenger begins with a demonstration that the device has an adverse impact on a group protected under Title VII. The challenger may use the Uniform Guidelines' "80 percent" rule. In some cases, challengers have used other measures, such as "statistical significance."

Once disparate impact is established, the employer must defend the selection device by showing that it is job-related. If the device is validated as job-related, then it will be held lawful, unless the challenger can show that there are alternative selection devices available to the employer that have less of a discriminatory effect on the employment of protected group members.

SELECTION FOR PROMOTIONS AND LAYOFFS

Use of selection devices to determine promotion and layoff decisions is subject to the same limitations as use of tests in hiring. If the device has an adverse impact on groups protected by Title VII, it must be validated or discarded. For example:

- An employer was found to have violated Title VII when, on the basis of low scores on its employee evaluation test, it laid off Spanish-surnamed employees. *(Brito v. Zia Co.)*
- In another case, a disproportionately high failure rate for black candidates compared to whites on one part of an employer's selection process for promotion was sufficient to establish a Title VII violation, despite the fact that overall the selection process did not have discriminatory results. *(Teal v. Connecticut)* The U.S. Supreme Court affirmed the appeals court determination that an employer charged with Title VII violations cannot rely on a "bottom line" defense showing that blacks as a group suffered no injury from the employer's job practices.

11
EMPLOYMENT CONDITIONS AND SENIORITY

The federal policy against employment discrimination based on race, color, religion, sex, or national origin extends to virtually every aspect of the employer-employee relationship.

The Title VII ban extends to discrimination with respect to "compensation, terms, conditions, or privileges of employment." Executive Order 11246 calls for affirmative action to provide equal employment opportunity in "employment, upgrading, demotion, or transfer; recruitment or recruitment advertising; layoff or termination; rates of pay or other forms of compensation; and selection for training, including apprenticeship."

An employer is free, however, to develop as many arbitrary, ridiculous, and irrational rules as it sees fit, provided that it applies them in an evenhanded, nondiscriminatory manner. (*Smith v. Monsanto Chemical Co.*)

The EEOC has found employers in violation of Title VII for condoning or neglecting to correct a variety of working conditions which were found to have a discriminatory effect on members of a protected class. Violations were found by the Commission where:

- The company's only black sales representative was assigned only to black accounts. (EEOC Decision No. 70350)
- An employer refused to hire a Spanish-surnamed American as a store manager on the basis of the applicant's appearance and accent peculiar to his national origin. (EEOC Decision No. AL 68-1-155E)

- Racial and ethnic jokes and derogatory restroom graffiti were tolerated along with an atmosphere of intimidation in the workplace. (EEOC Decision No. 74-05)
- Safety rules were applied disparately and it was shown that race was a factor in the administration of the rules. (EEOC Decision No. 71-1885)
- A racially prejudiced supervisor was retained, when the supervisor's presence was found not only to affect the terms and conditions of present employees but also the potential hiring of new black employees. (EEOC Decision No. 71-357)
- The use of Spanish during working as well as nonworking time was banned, when there was no demonstrable need for supervisors to understand all conversations among the Spanish-surnamed employees. (EEOC Decision No. 71-446)
- A black employee was discharged for a physical assault on his foreman, after continued racial intimidation and harassment of the employee by the foreman. (EEOC Decision No. 71-720)
- Standards of appearance and grooming for employees were enforced "without regard to their racially different physiological and cultural characteristics." (EEOC Decision No. 71-2444)

COMPENSATION

Employers cannot pay black employees less money than whites similarly situated, and they are liable for damages under Title VII, even if the discriminatory action began before the effective date of the Act, the Supreme Court ruled. *(Bazemore v. Friday)*

DEMOTIONS

Employers should not be able to avoid responsibility for discriminatory discharges by first demoting employees to part-time or fill-in status or by stringing out employees' tenures with nebulous commitments until employees must "quit" for their own economic well-being. (*Schneider v. Jax Shack, Inc.*)

SENIORITY

Title VII prohibits segregation by race, religion, sex, or national origin in collective bargaining units, lines of promotion, and seniority groups. An exception to Title VII permits discrimination that is based on a "bona fide" seniority system, as long as the system is not a guise for unlawful discrimination.

The question of discriminatory intent is relevant to whether the seniority system is bona fide under the Act, the Supreme Court has stated. (*Pullman-Standard v. Swint*)

Separate seniority rosters for white and black and male and female employees have been found to be violations of Title VII in such cases as *Griggs v. Duke Power Co.* and *United States v. Jacksonville Terminal Co.*

The key issue that has arisen regarding seniority is the impact of Title VII on seniority systems that had discriminated against minority groups prior to the passage of Title VII but were changed to employ "neutral" criteria from that point on. The question raised can be variously stated as:

- Can Title VII weaken or destroy the current and future seniority rights of white workers because such rights were earned under a seniority system that perpetuated the effects of discriminatory hiring practices?
- Can blacks be permanently locked into inferior positions because of seniority rights earned under such a system?

Similar questions have been raised regarding job referral systems of unions that formerly were all-white.

In two cases, the Supreme Court drastically modified the trend of decisions by the EEOC and by most appeals courts:

- In *Teamsters v. United States,* the Supreme Court ruled that seniority systems that may lock minorities into lower positions as the result of past discrimination are immune from attack under Title VII. The Court explained that it is not an unlawful employment practice for an employer to apply different employment standards pursuant to a bona fide seniority system as long as such differences are not the result of the intent to discriminate.

● In *United Airlines v. Evans*, the Court held that a seniority system that perpetuated the effects of a discriminatory discharge was valid. In this case, an employee had filed suit several years after the discharge, claiming that the denial of her seniority credit upon her rehire affected her present status. The Court explained in its decision that the charge should have been filed within the 90-day (180-day after the 1972 amendments) time period following the discriminatory practice. Without a timely charge, the Court held, post-Civil Rights Act discrimination is the legal equivalent of pre-Civil Rights Act discrimination.

Reading the two decisions together, it appears that under Title VII, seniority or merit systems may not be held to perpetuate discrimination which is not itself actionable, and that discrimination not timely complained of does not provide a cause of action. The cases completely rewrite the rules of affected class violations and relief under Title VII. No longer will there be countless class members including pre-Civil Rights Act as well as post-Civil Rights Act discriminatees.

The Supreme Court has also substantially limited the ability of minority workers to prevail in a challenge to a seniority practice currently in effect. The immunity from challenge granted by the 1964 Civil Rights Act to bona fide seniority systems is not limited to those in existence at the time of Title VII's enactment, the Court held in *American Tobacco Co. v. Patterson*, overturning an appeals court determination that a job promotion system requiring workers to progress from the lowest paid job in a department to the highest unlawfully discriminated against black employees at American Tobacco Company plants in Richmond, Virginia. Employees who challenge a seniority system must prove that it was established with a deliberate intent to discriminate, according to the Court. In this case, the Court concluded that limiting the immunity "to seniority systems in place prior to the effective date of the statute would be contrary to its plain language, inconsistent with our prior cases and would run counter to the national labor policy" favoring collective bargaining.

As a result of these decisions, employees will look to other laws to challenge seniority plans. The Civil Rights Act of 1866 provides one possible remedy, but it applies only to race and ethnic discrimination. Another avenue might be use of Executive Order 11246, which does not include the bona fide seniority exemption; the question remains whether the Order is a viable vehicle for remedying discrimination in those instances where use of Title VII is now foreclosed.

LAYOFFS

A particularly difficult issue is presented when a company that has discriminated in the past must lay off workers. The most common procedure used by companies in this position is to lay off the least senior workers ("last hired, first fired"). However, where the employer has discriminated against certain groups of workers in the past, the least senior workers will include a disproportionate number of people from those groups.

The "rightful place" doctrine would seem to prohibit displacing incumbent whites who are entitled, by virtue of their seniority rights, to keep their jobs. At the same time, the doctrine demands that past discrimination shall not adversely affect minority group rights when new employment decisions are made. Thus, the layoff situation presents major problems for courts that adhere to this view.

The Supreme Court has issued several major rulings in this area. In 1984, the Court held that Title VII does not permit the affirmative action goals of a consent decree benefiting employees who were not "actual victims" of discrimination to be given greater protection than a bona fide seniority system in the event of unanticipated layoffs.

The city of Memphis had proposed to lay off firefighters in accordance with its "last hired, first fired" seniority system. Federal courts had enjoined the city from following the seniority system because the proposed layoffs would have had a racially discriminatory effect under the terms of a hiring and promotion consent decree.

The Supreme Court said that only when "individual members" of a class can prove that they were "actual victims" of a discriminatory practice may they be awarded competitive seniority. The Court cited *Teamsters v. United States* for the proposition that "mere membership in the disadvantaged class is insufficient to warrant a seniority award." *(Firefighters, Local 1784 v. Stotts)*

Stotts had an immediate impact on lower courts. Within two months of the 1984 decision, two federal district courts decided that *Stotts* required them to reverse earlier rulings designed to protect members of minority groups from layoff. *(Vulcan Pioneers v. New Jersey Department of Civil Service; United States v. City of Cincinnati)*

However, in another post-*Stotts* decision, a federal district court ruled that the city of Detroit knowingly and intentionally breached its obligation to remedy past discrimination when it laid off black police officers pursuant to a collectively bargained seniority system—even though it knew such layoffs would wipe out most of the affirmative action recruiting which had brought large numbers of blacks into the department.

The city was ordered to reinstate illegally laid-off black officers who desired reinstatement, but the court also took measures to protect the interest of white officers with more seniority. The court based its ruling on the Fourteenth Amendment to the U.S. Constitution. *(NAACP v. Detroit Police Officers Association)*

In addition, an appeals court ruled that *Stotts* did not render invalid an affirmative action consent decree that includes goals for appointment and promotion of minority group individuals in civil service grades in the police force. *(Devereaux v. Geary)*

In 1986, the Supreme Court again faced the layoff issue. In a welter of separate opinions, the Court struck down a school board's "policy"—which had been included in a collective bargaining contract—of maintaining the racial proportions of the faculty or keeping the racial proportion of the faculty unchanged in making economic-based layoffs. Enough Justices wrote opinions favorable to various aspects of the concept of affirmative action, however, that it could be said that the case was a victory for supporters of an affirmative action that was wrapped in defeat. *(Wygant v. Jackson Board of Education)*

The *Wygant* decision may call into question an important appeals court ruling in which the Ninth Circuit rejected a challenge by seven white employees to a seniority override provision in a collective bargaining agreement. The contract called for an override of reverse seniority layoffs whenever reductions in force threatened the continued employment of specified numbers of women and minority workers. In *Tangren v. Wackenhut Services, Inc.* the court rejected the workers' Title VII challenge, holding that the voluntary contractual seniority override is permissible under the Supreme Court's decision in *Steelworkers v. Weber*.

12
REVERSE DISCRIMINATION AND RETALIATION

Through "reverse discrimination" complaints and lawsuits, white and/or male employees have been challenging employers' voluntary affirmative action programs intended to correct practices perceived as discriminatory.

Reverse discrimination charges have been used to attack a variety of affirmative action measures, including programs setting goals and timetables for recruiting, hiring, promoting, and training women and minority group persons, as well as modifications in layoff procedures. These legal challenges have resulted in employers questioning how they can comply with Title VII and the affirmative action requirements for federal contractors under Executive Order 11246, and still be protected from "reverse discrimination" charges.

EEOC GUIDELINES

The EEOC adopted guidelines, effective February 20, 1979, to protect employers and unions from charges of reverse discrimination when they voluntarily take action that is reasonably related to deficiencies disclosed by self-analysis (401 FEP Manual 225).

The EEOC's affirmative action guidelines also state that a federal contractor's compliance with the affirmative action requirements of Executive Order 11246 is lawful under Title VII.

The guidelines also state that "interim goals or targets for previously excluded groups may be higher than the percentage of their availability in the workforce so that the long-term goal may be met in a reasonable period of time." According to the guidelines, "in order to achieve such interim goals, an employer may consider race, sex, or national origin in making selections among qualified or qualifiable applicants."

WYGANT AND *SHEET METAL WORKERS* CASES

In *Wygant v. Jackson Board of Education,* the Supreme Court struck down the school board's policy of maintaining the racial proportions of the faculty in making economic-based layoffs. Justice Powell, joined by Chief Justice Burger and Justice Rehnquist, took the position that affirmative action by a public employer has to be "narrowly tailored." That standard was not met, he declared, on the basis of assertions that the school board was remedying societal discrimination and was ensuring that minority group students would have black role models with whom they could identify. There had been no determination that the school board had engaged in discrimination, Powell observed, and yet the board was laying off white teachers with more seniority than the minority group teachers who were being retained.

In *Local 28, Sheet Metal Workers v. EEOC,* the Supreme Court held that district courts had the power to order affirmative, race-conscious relief when necessary to counteract "egregious discrimination." The union, joined by the United States, unsuccessfully argued that a court's imposition of membership goals and preferences for nonwhites were prohibited by the Act. Justice Brennan stated that the Act does not say that a court may order relief only for the actual victims of discrimination.

WEBER AND *BAKKE* CASES

In *Steelworkers v. Weber,* the Supreme Court ruled that private employers can legally give special preference to black workers to eliminate "manifest racial imbalance" in historically white-only jobs. Upholding an agreement between an employer and a union that reserved 50 percent of the openings in inplant craft training programs for black employees until the percentage of black craft workers in the plant corresponded to the percentage of blacks in the local labor force, the Court said this arrangement "falls within the area of discretion left by Title VII to the private sector voluntarily to adopt affirmative action plans designed to eliminate conspicuous racial imbalance in traditionally segregated job categories."

The Court made the following rulings en route to its conclusions:

- Judicial findings of exclusion of blacks from craft jobs on racial grounds are so numerous that such exclusion is a proper subject for judicial notice.
- Title VII's prohibition against racial discrimination does not concern all private, voluntary, race-conscious affirmative action plans, since this prohibition must be read against the background of the legislative history of the 1964 Civil Rights Act and the historical context from which Title VII arose. A literal interpretation of the statute would bring about an end completely at variance with the purpose of the statute, which was to integrate blacks into the mainstream of American society.
- Section 703(j) of the Act, which provides that nothing in Title VII requires an employer to grant preferential treatment to correct racial imbalance, does not mean that all voluntary, race-conscious affirmative action is forbidden, and the "natural inference" is that Congress chose not to forbid such efforts.
- The line of demarcation between permissible and impermissible affirmative action plans need not be defined in detail in the case. The challenged plan falls on the permissible side of the line; it does not require the discharge of white workers and their replacement with new black hires, does not create an absolute bar to the advancement of white employees, and is a temporary measure that will end when a manifest racial imbalance is eliminated.

However, the degree to which an employer's voluntary affirmative action efforts must be formal and specific in order to survive reverse discrimination challenges under Title VII remains an unresolved question under *Weber*. There have been several significant post-*Weber* cases:

- An employer's court-ordered grant of remedial seniority to black employees did not constitute reverse discrimination. *(Moseley v. Goodyear Tire & Rubber Co.)*
- Title VII does not require an employer to promote every black employee who participates in an affirmative action training program. *(Wright v. National Archives & Records Service)*
- A voluntary action program was "clearly permissible" under the standards laid down in *Weber*, a federal district court ruled. *(Edmondson v. United States Steel Corp.)*

A prima facie case of reverse discrimination is established on showing that background circumstances support the suspicion that an employer is the unusual employer that discriminates against the majority and on showing that an employer treated differently employees who were similarly situated but not members of a protected group. *(Parker v. Baltimore & Ohio R.R.)*

Before *Weber*, in *Regents of University of California v. Bakke*, the Supreme Court found that a University of California affirmative action program violated Title VI of the Civil Rights Act of 1964 by maintaining a special admissions procedure that excluded white applicants from 16 percent of the first-year medical school class. Nevertheless, the Court also said that a school may establish an affirmative action program that considers race as one of the factors in admission. Because the *Bakke* decision was made in an educational context rather than an employment one, the meaning of the ruling for employers remains unclear.

RETALIATION

Like some of the other major federal labor laws, including the Taft-Hartley and Fair Labors Standards Acts, Title VII contains a prohibition against retaliation. Section 704(a) makes it an unlawful employment practice to discriminate against any employee, union member or applicant for employment or union membership because he or she has opposed an unlawful employment practice or has filed a charge, testified, assisted, or participated in any manner in an investigation, proceeding, or hearing under Title VII. The prohibition applies to employers, employment agencies, labor unions, and joint labor-management committees controlling apprenticeship or other training or retraining programs.

Injunctive Relief

The provisions forbidding retaliatory action are not self-enforcing. For this reason, in the 1972 amendments Congress gave the EEOC and the attorney general authority to seek temporary injunctive relief to preserve the status quo where there is an allegation of unlawful retaliatory action. But the Fifth Circuit held that the 1972 amendment did not take away the pre-existing right of an employee to go into court and seek such relief on his or her own, based on an allegation of retaliatory action taken because the employee filed a charge with the EEOC. (*Drew v. Liberty Mutual Insurance Co.*)

Scope of Protection

According to the Fifth Circuit, a person filing charges of discrimination against his or her employer is protected against retaliation even if those charges are false or malicious. (*Pettway v. American Cast Iron Pipe Co.*)

But the First Circuit decided that the protection against retaliation under Section 704(a) does not give an employee unlimited license to file a complaint of alleged discrimination. Upholding a lower court finding that the employee's discharge was not a violation, the court explained that a balance must be reached between the purpose of protecting persons engaging reasonably in activities opposing discrimination and in Congress' equally manifest desire not to tie the hands of employers in objective selection and control of personnel. (*Hochstadt v. Worcester Foundation*)

Examples of Retaliation

In the eyes of the EEOC, retaliation violations are particularly serious, first because they work a great hardship upon the individual involved, and second because they have a long-term chilling effect upon the willingness of others to oppose Title VII discrimination. For this reason, the EEOC and the courts have construed this protection broadly. Here are some examples of holdings on retaliation:

- An employer engaged in unlawful retaliation by refusing to process an employment application until the applicant, who had filed a charge with the EEOC against another company, settled his dispute with that company. *(Barela v. United Nuclear Corp.)*
- An employer violated Title VII by harassing an employee who had filed a charge with the EEOC, directing supervisors to build a case against her and to apply a pattern of oppressive supervision over her. *(Francis v. AT&T)*
- A violation was found when a medical clinic, after being ordered by Medicaid officials to integrate its segregated patient reception and waiting rooms, discharged the sole black receptionist when the integration permitted a reduction of one employee in the number of receptionists required. (EEOC Decision No. 72-1267)
- An employer was held to have engaged in unlawful discrimination where an employee who filed a charge against the employer thereafter was assigned to "erratic and undesirable working hours." (EEOC Decision No. 72-0455)
- In two separate cases, violations were found where employees were discharged for objecting to (1) a supervisor harassing employees by preaching on the job, and (2) a company's mandatory religious meetings. (EEOC Decision Nos. 72-1114, 72-0528)

PART 4

ADMINISTRATION AND ENFORCEMENT

13
TITLE VII:
EEOC PROCEEDINGS

There are two methods for instituting an administrative proceeding before the EEOC:

- First, a charge may be filed in writing and under oath by or on behalf of a person claiming to be aggrieved.
- Second, a written charge may be filed by an EEOC member who has reasonable cause to believe that a violation has occurred. Such a charge also must be sworn to.

Many of the states and municipalities have laws or ordinances forbidding the same types of discrimination in employment as are specified in Title VII. To give state and local agencies the first opportunity to resolve some of the issues involving an alleged case of discrimination, Title VII provides that no charge may be filed with the EEOC by an aggrieved person for 60 days after proceedings have been started under state or local law or for 60 days after termination of such proceedings, whichever occurs first. If a state or municipality has a new law, the EEOC deferral period is extended to 120 days.

This deferral policy was intended to support and encourage the operation of the state agencies; it was not intended to complicate the filing of complaints. Title VII also states that no charge may be filed with the EEOC without first going to the state or local agency. In this regard, the Supreme Court has approved the EEOC's practice of accepting a charge, orally referring it to the state or local agency on behalf of the charging party, and then beginning to process it upon expiration of the deferral period without requiring the filing of a new charge. (*Love v. Pullman Co.*)

The EEOC is required to accord "substantial weight" to the final findings and orders of state and local agencies. But the EEOC will designate as appropriate "deferral agencies"—state and local agencies to which it will grant primary jurisdiction—only those whose laws prohibit essentially all the practices by essentially all the types of persons on essentially all the grounds covered by Title VII.

EEOC PROCESSING OF CHARGES

Title VII sets out the following procedural steps for processing a charge:
- A charge must be filed within 180 days of the occurrence of the alleged unlawful employment practice. (If a charge is filed initially with the state or local agency within the 180 days, the charge must be filed with the EEOC within 300 days of the occurrence or within 30 days after receipt of a notice that the state or local agency has terminated its proceedings, whichever occurs first. (*Mohasco Corp. v. Silver*)
- After a charge is filed (or once the state or local deferral is ended), the EEOC must serve a notice of the charge on the respondent within 10 days.
- The EEOC must then investigate the charge to determine whether there is reasonable cause to believe it is true.
- The Commission must make its determination of reasonable cause as promptly as possible and, so far as practicable, within 120 days.
- If it finds no reasonable cause, the Commission must dismiss the charge; if it finds reasonable cause, it will attempt to conciliate.
- If the Commission is unable to secure a conciliation agreement that is acceptable to it within 30 days, it may bring a civil action in an appropriate U.S. district court.
- If the EEOC does not bring an action within 180 days, it will issue a "right to sue" letter, notifying the complaining party that the person has 90 days to file suit in federal

court on his or her own behalf. The EEOC may also issue a notice of "right to sue" upon an aggrieved party's request after 180 days have elapsed since the date of the filing of the charge with the Commission. Nevertheless, the EEOC has a continuous right to file a Title VII action in federal court against the employer, even after the 180-day period and issuance of notice of "right to sue." *(EEOC v. Occidental Life Insurance Co. of California)*

The EEOC is strictly required to go through all of the procedures specified by the 1964 Civil Rights Act before filing suit of its own in federal district court. Failure to do so is grounds for dismissing the EEOC's case. Failure of the Commission to follow EEOC or Title VII procedural regulations usually is not sufficient grounds, however, for dismissal of an employee's federal court action. The reasoning in this regard is that individuals should not be penalized for the acts of omissions of the Commission.

It has also been held that failure by the EEOC to follow its own regulations for initiating lawsuits, as opposed to Title VII requirements, can be grounds for dismissing the Commission's suit. Thus, one court of appeals found that the EEOC's failure to follow its regulation requiring it to give notice of termination of conciliation efforts to an employer that had refused to participate, warranted dismissal of the Title VII action against the employer. The court emphasized that the EEOC regulation not followed was more than a technicality, in light of the central role of conciliation in the Title VII scheme. *(EEOC v. Hickey-Mitchell Co.)*

Timely filing of a charge with the EEOC is not a jurisdictional prerequisite for a Title VII action. *(Zipes v. Trans World Airlines)*

The EEOC has the same investigative authority under the 1964 Civil Rights Act as the NLRB has under the Taft-Hartley Act. This means that the EEOC has broad rights of access to documentary evidence and of summoning witnesses and taking testimony. It also has the right to seek the assistance of U.S. district courts in compelling the production of evidence and the attendance of witnesses. The Commission, its officials, and its employees are under congressional injunction not to make public any information uncovered in the course of investigations.

Aggrieved Person

The "aggrieved individual" who is entitled to file a charge of discrimination is defined very broadly by the EEOC and the courts. The term has been held to include:

- A white female employee who claimed to have suffered from loss of benefits from lack of association with racial minorities at work *(EEOC v. Bailey Co.)*

- An organization concerned with the rights of female employees, suing on behalf of a female former employee *(EEOC v. Rinella & Rinella)*

- A civil rights organization, through its attorney, suing on behalf of its members and a class of black employees *(EEOC v. Jackson Coca Cola Bottling Co.)*

INTERPRETATIVE GUIDELINES

In addition to its power to issue procedural regulations, the Commission has authority to issue and publicize its interpretations of Title VII provisions. The U.S. Supreme Court has held that the Commission's interpretative guidelines are entitled to "some deference." *(Hardison v. Trans World Airlines, Inc.)* However, most courts have failed to interpret the EEOC's guidelines as legal obligations of employers.

EEOC Opinion Letters

In reply to inquiries from employers or unions regarding the applicability of Title VII to particular situations, the EEOC or its General Counsel issues letters to the inquiring parties giving the Commission's views on the questions presented. The EEOC has ruled that such letters can be relied on only by the addressee, and that they have no effect upon situations other than those of the specific addressee.

EEOC Decisions

Beginning in mid-1969, the EEOC began releasing for publication selected decisions written by the Commission on whether reasonable cause exists to credit particular charges of Title VII violations. Names and other identifying data are deleted from such decisions, since the statute bars the Commission from identifying the parties to conciliation proceedings before it.

PROVING DISCRIMINATION

How does an individual prove that an employer or union unlawfully discriminated against him or her? How does an employer or union rebut such a claim?

The initial burden to provide evidence is on the plaintiff. But once he or she shows a prima facie case, the burden of rebutting the presumption of discrimination shifts to the employer or other respondent, who must show that the action which is the basis of the charge was taken for nondiscriminatory reasons. Even if the respondent presents such evidence, the charging party may reply with the assertion that the reasons stated by the respondent were pretextual and that the underlying reason was discriminatory.

Basic Rules

In *McDonnell Douglas Corp. v. Green*, a leading case decided in 1973, the Supreme Court held that a black applicant made a prima facie case of discrimination by showing:
- He was black.
- He applied for a vacant job for which he was qualified.
- He was rejected.
- The employer continued to seek applicants for the job after he was rejected.

In an attempt to rebut the prima facie case, the employer presented evidence of the applicant's participation in an illegal stall-in in front of the plant for which he was arrested and convicted. The Court said this was sufficient rebuttal of the prima facie case.

But the Court did not stop there. The applicant, it added had the right to show that the reasons for rejection advanced by the employer were pretextual—a "cover-up" for a racially discriminatory decision.

To show the justification advanced by the employer was a pretext, the Court continued, the employee could demonstrate (1) that others similarly situated were not refused employment, (2) the employer's treatment of the employee during previous employment, (3) the employer's reaction to the applicant's previous civil rights activity, and (4) the employer's "general policy and practice with respect to minority employment."

Regarding point 4, the Court said: "Statistics as to petitioner's employment policy and practice may be helpful to a determination of whether petitioner's refusal to rehire respondent in this case conformed to a general pattern of discrimination against blacks."

Use of Statistics

The Supreme Court elaborated on the *Green* doctrine in two cases decided in 1977. Although statistics may be used to prove racially discriminatory hiring practices, the Court said in the first case, *Hazelwood School District v. United States*, that the employer (a school district) has the right to have recent hiring practices considered to counter the proof of discrimination. An employer making all employment decisions in a wholly nondiscriminatory way from the date it became subject to Title VII could not be held to have violated the 1964 Civil Rights Act even if it formerly had maintained an all-white work force by purposefully excluding blacks, the Court said.

In reviewing the appeals court decision in the case, the Supreme Court said the lower court "totally disregarded the possibility" that the finding of discrimination might be rebutted by statistics concerning the school district's hiring practices after it was made subject to Title VII by the 1972 amendments. The Court remanded the case for a more refined statistical analysis of the relevant labor market.

In the second case, *Teamsters v. United States*, the Court added these principles to the use of statistics to prove violations:

- Statistics showing a racial imbalance in the composition of the employer's work force as compared with the composition of the population of the community from which the workers are hired are of probative value in a case alleging racial discrimination.
- It is ordinarily expected that over time nondiscriminatory hiring practices will result in a work force more or less representative of the racial composition of the community. However, considerations such as the small size of the sample and evidence showing that figures for the general population might not accurately reflect the pool of qualified job applicants also would be relevant.

In 1986, the Supreme Court decided another case involving the issue of statistics, *Bazemore v. Friday*. In *Bazemore*, the Court held that regression analysis that includes less than "all measurable variables" may serve to prove a Title VII claim since the preponderance of evidence, not scientific certainty, is the standard of proof.

CONCILIATION PROCEEDINGS

Under Title VII, special emphasis is placed on conciliation where there are charges of discrimination.

Title VII allows 30 days for the EEOC to work out a conciliation agreement between the parties before a suit may be brought. Nothing said or done during the attempt to achieve voluntary compliance may be made public without the written consent of the parties. Nor may it be used in a subsequent court action. The conciliation procedure is as follows:

- After the Commission decides that there is cause to believe that discrimination has occurred, the Director of Compliance notifies the charging party and the respondent that a conciliator will contact them to resolve the dispute.
- The conciliator first meets with the charging party to determine what remedy would be satisfactory, then tries to persuade the respondent to accept a remedy acceptable to the charging party and the EEOC.

- If accepted by the respondents, the remedy is embodied in a conciliation agreement that is signed by the charging party and the respondent and submitted to the EEOC for approval.
- If the respondent fails or refuses to conciliate or to make a good-faith effort to resolve the dispute, the EEOC may terminate its conciliation efforts and so notify the respondent. Conciliation efforts will not be resumed except upon a written request from the respondent within a specified period.
- If the EEOC terminates the conciliation procedure without providing the notification called for by its regulations, a subsequent suit by the EEOC against the employer may be subject to dismissal.
- In addition to remedying the charging party's individual complaint, the EEOC normally attempts to include in the conciliation agreement modifications of other employment practices to bring them into compliance with Title VII. This could involve inclusion of an affirmative action program.

There is no public policy reason for permitting an employer that entered into an EEOC conciliation agreement containing seniority provisions in conflict with those of a collective bargaining contract to escape contractual liability to male employees who were laid off under the conciliation agreement's seniority provision, the Supreme Court ruled. *(W.R. Grace & Co. v. Rubber Workers)*

SETTLEMENT AGREEMENTS

To avoid lengthy and costly court enforcement or contract debarment proceedings, the EEOC, the OFCCP, and the Justice Department have negotiated settlement agreements with major companies, industries, and public sector employees. Agreements include the following:

- The first settlement agreement was reached in January 1973 with the American Telephone and Telegraph Company and its then 24 operating companies. Without admitting any violations, the companies agreed to pay about $15 million to 13,000 women and 2,000 men who were members of minority groups who had been denied pay and promotion opportunities. In addition, the companies agreed to develop goals for increasing the utilization of women and minorities in each job classification in all 700 establishments within the Bell System.

- A second settlement of national significance was reached the following year between the government—the EEOC and the Justice Department—and nine major steel companies and the United Steelworkers Union. In addition to providing back pay for 40,000 employees, the agreement set goals and timetables for filling openings in trade and craft jobs with women and minority group employees. The settlement was upheld in *United States v. Allegheny-Ludlum Industries, Inc.*

- A third settlement of a major action was signed in June 1978 between General Electric and the EEOC. The conciliation agreement, which GE said would cost up to $32 million over five years, resolved a 1973 action charging it with systematic employment discrimination against women and members of minority groups.

- In 1983, the EEOC and Burlington Northern, Inc., one of the nation's largest rail carriers, reached an agreement that provided $10 million in back pay to alleged victims of race discrimination. Along with back pay, the settlement provides that rejected black applicants who reapply for jobs with the company within six years be given priority consideration. The approximately 5,000 jobs that will be offered represent an estimated value of $40 million, according to the EEOC.

- Also in 1983, the EEOC and General Motors Corp. signed a record-setting $42 million agreement that settled a decade-old bias charge against the auto maker.

The cornerstone of the accord calls for a program providing $15 million in grants and endowments for 28 designated colleges and for educational assistance programs. Minority and women class members who are GM employees, including those on layoff, are eligible to participate in the program.

- In the public sector, the Justice Department has obtained several major back pay awards in consent decrees. In April 1982, Fairfax County, Va., agreed to pay $2.7 million in back pay to 685 individuals whom the Justice Department claimed had been denied employment by the county because of their sex or race.

SUITS BY THE EEOC, ATTORNEY GENERAL

Under the 1972 amendments, the EEOC, if it is unable to secure an acceptable conciliation agreement within 30 days after filing of the charge or after the expiration of the state agency deferral period, may bring an action against the respondent in a federal district court. In cases against a state or local government, the attorney general, rather than the EEOC, is authorized to bring the action. The individual also retains the right to bring a court action if he or she is dissatisfied with the EEOC's handling of the case. In 1984, the EEOC adopted a new policy calling for litigation consideration of every case in which conciliation efforts failed. However, there is disagreement among the appeals courts concerning the EEOC's right to bring suit if a suit based on the same charge already has been brought by the individual.

Time Limits on EEOC Suits

The EEOC's right to sue is not confined by a time limit, the U.S. Supreme Court has ruled. The 180-day period referred to in Section 706(f)(1) of Title VII means, the Court explained, what it says, "that an aggrieved person unwilling to await the conclusion of extended EEOC proceedings may institute a private lawsuit within 180 days after the charge has been filed. The section does not impose a limit on EEOC." *(Occidental Life Insurance Co. v. EEOC)*

The EEOC and Class Actions

Rule 23 of the Federal Rules of Civil Procedure requires that a class action brought in a federal court be certified by the court prior to a hearing on the merits of the claims. If the group of individuals forming the class cannot meet the requirements set out for class certification in Rule 23, the court will dismiss the suit as a class action. However, the Supreme Court has ruled that the EEOC may seek classwide relief without complying with Rule 23. *(General Telephone Co. of the Northwest v. EEOC)*

Class Certification

The Supreme Court has issued several decisions regarding class certification:

- The Court held that a discrimination charge, brought by three Mexican-Americans challenging a trucking company's "no transfer" and seniority policies should not have been certified as a class action by the appeals court. Although agreeing that racial and ethnic bias suits are often by their nature class action suits, the Court explained that the three employees were not adequate representatives of the class of victims of discrimination. None were qualified for the positions denied, and they stipulated that they had not been discriminated against when they were hired. In addition, the Court noted that they had failed to request certification of the class before trial. *(East Texas Motor Freight System v. Rodriguez)*

- The Court also ruled that a Mexican-American employee's claim that he was discriminatorily denied promotion does not entitle him to represent either a class of other Mexican-American employees who were denied promotion or a class of Mexican-American job applicants. *(General Telephone Co. of the Southwest v. Falcon)*

- A former employee who receives a notice of right to sue while a class certification motion is pending in an existing Title VII case may wait until this motion is denied before bringing his or her own Title VII action, the Supreme Court has held. *(Crown, Cork & Seal Co. v. Parker)*

- On the other hand, the Supreme Court also held that a judgment against a class of employees who alleged a pattern or practice of racial discrimination does not preclude individual employees, who are members of the class, from maintaining subsequent actions against the employer alleging individual claims of racial discrimination. *(Cooper v. Federal Reserve Bank of Richmond)*

Subpoena Authority

The Supreme Court has ruled that a charge meeting the requirements of Title VII is a jurisdictional prerequisite for judicial enforcement of an EEOC subpoena. The Court also ruled that the EEOC is required to furnish notice to the party that includes all the information in the charge itself, but the agency does not have to supply notice that is more informative than the charge itself. *(EEOC v. Shell Oil Co.)*

Pattern or Practice Cases

Under the 1964 Civil Rights Act, the attorney general was given authority to seek an injunction where he had "reasonable cause" to believe that individuals were engaged in a "pattern or practice of resistance" to the rights protected by Title VII. The 1972 amendments transferred this jurisdiction to the EEOC, effective two years later. On certification that the case is of general public importance, a three-judge court may be convened. The case must be assigned for a hearing at the earliest practical date and must be expedited in every way. Appeal from the judgment of the three-judge court may be taken directly to the Supreme Court.

SUITS BY INDIVIDUALS

Several questions have been raised regarding the right of an individual to go into court on his or her own behalf:
- Must that individual have filed a charge with the EEOC?
- Is it necessary that he or she wait until the EEOC makes an attempt at conciliation?
- Must the individual also wait until the EEOC finds reasonable cause to believe that the charge has merit?
- Apart from the need to pursue his or her remedies before the EEOC, should the individual be required to pursue

any available remedies under an applicable collective bargaining contract? And if the individual does so and loses, may he or she nevertheless file a suit in court under Title VII based on the same claim?

● A related question is whether an individual's decision to pursue his or her remedies before a state or local FEP agency or under a union contract operates to "toll" (suspend) the time limits for bringing court action under Title VII.

Court decisions on such jurisdictional issues are discussed below.

Filing of Charges

The Supreme Court has ruled that the filing of a timely charge with the EEOC is not a jurisdictional prerequisite to the maintenance of a Title VII action, but is instead a requirement that, like a statute of limitations, is subject to waiver, estoppel, and equitable tolling. (*Zipes v. Trans World Airlines*)

In general, courts have shown some reluctance to dismiss a complaint merely because the plaintiff has not proceeded properly before the EEOC. However, the filing of a charge with the EEOC generally is held to be a prerequisite to filing a court suit. (*Stebbins v. Nationwide Mutual Insurance Co.*) And an employee who did not file timely EEOC charges cannot rely on another person's charge that was not timely as to that person's own claims, even though the charge would be timely as to the employee's claim. (*Allen v. United States Steel Corp.*)

Contractual Remedies

When an individual has contractual remedies available, the courts generally have ruled that the contractual grievance procedure need not be pursued before a suit may be brought under Title VII. While acknowledging that this may place the burden of a double defense on an employer, an appeals court noted that there might be differences in the processes and remedies afforded by each. But it held that after pursuing both remedies, the employee must elect one in order to preclude duplicate relief, "which would result in an unjust enrichment or windfall to the plaintiffs." *(Bowe v. Colgate Palmolive Co.)*

Conciliation by EEOC

Conciliation efforts by the EEOC are not a jurisdictional prerequisite to the bringing of a Title VII suit by an individual, several appeals courts have held. Title VII merely requires that the Commission have an opportunity to persuade the employer or union before the action could be brought. *(Brown v. Gaston County Dyeing Machine Co.)*

Reasonable Cause Finding

The absence of an EEOC determination of "reasonable cause" does not bar suit under the appropriate section of Title VII, the Supreme Court has held. *(McDonnell Douglas Corp. v. Green)*

Tolling of Time Periods

Under Title VII, an individual is required to bring suit within 90 days of receipt of the EEOC's notice of right to sue. Two interpretive problems are raised by this provision: what constitutes notice of right to sue and what constitutes bringing a suit?

Under the EEOC's present policy, charging parties receive only one letter from it. This letter announces conciliation efforts have failed and gives notice of the right to sue. It is sent, not following the failure of conciliation, but rather following the investigation of the charge by the General Counsel.

The Supreme Court has ruled that a race discrimination claimant who filed her EEOC right-to-sue notice with a federal district court within 90 days of receiving the notice from the EEOC—but failed to file a formal complaint—did not comply with the limitations period contained in Title VII. *(Baldwin County Welcome Center v. Brown)*

Adverse Local Rulings

The Supreme Court has said that Title VII does not require claimants to pursue in state court an unfavorable state administrative decision. However, the Court also said that a former employee who first alleged religious and national origin discrimination in an EEOC charge and who, upon being referred to a state FEP agency, was obligated—if he desired to raise an allegation of national origin discrimination in a Title VII action—first to bring it before the state agency.

Also, in the same case, the Court held that a state court decision upholding a state FEP agency's rejection of a former employee's claim of employment discrimination as meritless bars the former employee from suing under Title VII. (*Kremer v. Chemical Construction Corp.*)

The Supreme Court also has ruled that Congress did not intend unreviewed state administrative proceedings to have a preclusive effect on Title VII claims, whether or not the Title VII claimant requested an administrative hearing or was compelled to participate in it. (*University of Tennessee v. Elliott*)

Arbitration

An employee who has submitted his or her grievance to final arbitration under the nondiscrimination clause of a union contract does not relinquish the statutory right to go into court under Title VII to redress a discrimination complaint, the U.S. Supreme Court has held. Neither the doctrine of election of remedies, nor the doctrine of waiver, nor the federal labor policy respecting arbitration bars the employee whose claim of racial discrimination was rejected by an arbitrator from bringing an action under Title VII. The Court added that federal courts are not required to defer to the arbitrator's decision but instead should consider the employee's claim de novo. (*Alexander v. Gardner-Denver Co.*)

A further issue raised when an employee uses the grievance-arbitration forum is whether the time spent during the grievance-arbitration process is to be counted in computing, for purposes of determining compliance with the statue of limitations, how much time the employee took to file with the EEOC. The U.S. Supreme Court ruled, after much confusion in the appeals courts, that rights under Title VII and rights under the collective bargaining agreement are independent and that what happens in arbitration should not affect the Title VII adjudication process. Because the two actions are independent and can be pursued concurrently, the Court held that grievance arbitration proceedings do not "toll" the Title VII limitations period. *(Electrical Workers, Local 790 v. Robbins & Myers, Inc.)*

14
TITLE VII:
JUDICIAL RELIEF

The remedial provisions of Title VII are intended to provide broad and effective remedies for violations of the 1964 Civil Rights Act's prohibitions. In addition to prohibiting the unlawful employment practice and requiring institution of such affirmative action as may be necessary and appropriate, courts increasingly have found back pay and attorneys' fees appropriate to compensate victims of employment discrimination. Under the 1972 amendments, back pay is limited to no more than the amount that accrued during the two years prior to the filing of the charge. In some instances, the courts also have found it appropriate to award punitive damages where compensatory damages either were not applicable or were not regarded as sufficient.

REMEDYING PAST BIAS

In 1986, the Supreme Court issued several rulings on the issue of remedying past bias.

In one case, the Court held that district courts had the power to order affirmative, race-conscious relief when necessary to counteract "egregious discrimination." The Sheet Metal Workers, joined by the United States, unsuccessfully argued that a court's imposition of membership goals and preferences for nonwhites were prohibited by the Act. Justice Brennan stated that the Act does not say that a court may order relief only for the actual victims of discrimination. (*Local 28, Sheet Metal Workers v. EEOC*)

In another case, the Court ruled that voluntary action available to employers and unions seeking to eradicate racial discrimination may include race-conscious relief that benefits individuals who were not actual victims of discrimination, regardless of whether voluntary action occurs in the context of a consent decree or entirely outside the context of litigation. *(Local 93, Firefighters v. City of Cleveland)*

These two decisions cast doubt on the viability of a 1984 ruling, in which the Supreme Court held that Title VII does not permit the affirmative action goals of a consent decree benefiting employees who were not "actual victims" of discrimination to be given greater protection than a bona fide seniority system in the event of unanticipated layoffs. As a result of the decree, some white employees with more seniority than black employees were laid off or demoted. The Court said that there had been no finding by a court that the black employees protected from layoff under the consent decree had been victims of discrimination. *(Firefighters, Local 1784 v. Stotts)*

Subsequent to these rulings, the Supreme Court affirmed that a federal district court was not required to allow white troopers to present evidence on the "harsh impact" that the imposition of promotion quotas would have on them when the quota order was consistent with the purposes of Title VII, did not unnecessarily trammel the interests of the white troopers, did not absolutely bar advancement to corporal, and was a temporary measure. *(United States v. Paradise)*

Prior to *Stotts*, courts grappled with this issue in the following ways:

- Retroactive seniority dating to the employee's original application was awarded to minority group truck drivers who were discriminated against because of race. Such relief is an appropriate remedy under Title VII, the Supreme Court said, noting that back pay alone is not sufficient to "make whole" the victims of past discrimination. In answer to a charge that such seniority would unfairly penalize "innocent" white workers, the Court responded that there must be a "sharing of the burden" of the past discrimination. *(Franks v. Bowman Transportation Co.)*

The Supreme Court also ruled that a settlement properly awarded retroactive seniority to persons whose claims were time-barred as well as those with timely claims. Retroactive seniority contrary to a labor contract may be awarded despite the objections of a contracting union which has not itself been found guilty of discrimination. *(Zipes v. Trans World Airlines)*

- A court of appeals ordered a fire department to institute a hiring plan giving absolute job preference to 20 minority applicants for the next 40 vacancies. *(Carter v. Gallagher)*
- Another court of appeals approved the use of hiring ratios in affirming an order requiring that firefighters who passed a validated test should be placed into separate pools of whites, blacks, and Spanish-surnamed persons and be hired according to specified ratios until each fire department had a percentage of minority group firefighters approximately equal to the percentage of minority group persons in the locality. *(Boston Chapter, NAACP v. Beecher)*
- The use of quotas was rejected as a method of determining promotions in a state corrections department, except as an interim measure to be used until nondiscriminatory promotion procedures were developed. The appeals court ruling included this strong anti-quota language: "No one should be bumped from a preferred position on the eligibility list solely because of his race. Unless the Fourteenth Amendment is applicable only to blacks, this is constitutionally forbidden reverse discrimination." *(Kirkland v. New York State Department of Correctional Services)*

DAMAGES

The courts are divided on whether Title VII authorizes the award of exemplary compensatory damages in addition to back pay and attorneys' fees. A split of authority also exists on the question of whether Title VII authorizes the award of punitive damages, but the majority view seems to be that such a remedy is not available. One appeals court, for example, rejected the remedy of punitive damages in the Title VII context. The court found nothing in Title VII that would authorize an award of punitive damages, and noted that had Congress meant to provide for this remedy it would have done so explicitly. *(EEOC v. Detroit Edison Co.)*

BACK PAY AWARDS

Under the 1972 amendments, back pay liability under Title VII may not exceed that accruing from a date more than two years prior to the filing of the charge. The legislative history indicates that this limitation on back pay was intended "to give the court wide discretion, as has been generally exercised by the courts under existing law, in fashioning the most complete relief possible." A discussion of some of the issues in this area follows:

- The Supreme Court has held that ordinarily a plaintiff who successfully obtains an injunction under Title VII should be awarded back pay as well. The Court said that back pay should be denied to victims of discrimination only for reasons that, if applied generally, would not frustrate the central purposes of Title VII. Applying this rule, the Court found that the absence of bad faith on the part of a Title VII defendant is not sufficient reason for denying back pay. Plaintiffs need to be compensated for the effects of discrimination whether or not the discrimination was intentional, the Court explained. *(Albemarle Paper Co. v. Moody)*

The Supreme Court has ruled that a rejected job applicant's duty to minimize damages requires him or her to accept an offer he or she originally sought, even if the offer does not include retroactive seniority. Rejection of such a job offer tolls the running of the back-pay period, the Court said. *(Ford Motor Co. v. EEOC)*

- When the plaintiff brings a class action suit against an employer, all those who are victims of discriminatory practices or policies may be included in the class receiving back pay, whether or not they have filed charges with the EEOC. *(Robinson v. P. Lorillard Co.)* In a class action suit for back pay, notice of the suit must be given to each member of the class, and individual plaintiffs may not opt out of it.

- States found guilty of discrimination are not protected from awards of money damages by the doctrine of sovereign immunity, the Supreme Court has ruled. The 1972 amendments which extended Title VII protections to state and local governmental employees also extend remedies such as back pay and attorneys' fees. Rejecting the argument that such awards should not be permitted against a state because they would drain the state treasury, the Supreme Court held that the equal protection clause of the Fourteenth Amendment to the Constitution granted Congress the power to amend Title VII to require states, as well as other employers guilty of discrimination, to pay back pay and attorneys' fees. *(Fitzpatrick v. Bitzer)*
- A female police department employee who was unlawfully denied a police officer post because of her sex was entitled to back pay under Title VII for several years beyond the date that she voluntarily resigned from the department, an appeals court ruled. *(Thorne v. City of El Segundo)*

ATTORNEYS' FEES

Title VII allows courts discretion to award reasonable attorneys' fees to prevailing parties—plaintiff or defendant. But what is a "prevailing party"? One court of appeals has held that a federal employee who had prevailed on an interlocutory appeal from an order requiring her to exhaust administrative remedies before proceeding further with her Title VII action was not entitled to attorneys' fees because she had not yet proven discrimination and therefore was not the prevailing party within the meaning of the 1964 Civil Rights Act. The court found her claim premature, explaining that Congress could not have intended that fees be assessed against a defendant absent any showing of discrimination. *(Grubbs v. Butz)*

Although Title VII provides for awards to either a plaintiff or a defendant, awards of attorneys' fees to prevailing defendants against private plaintiffs are not the general rule, in view of the congressional priority given to vindicating the rights of complaining employees and the likelihood that the employees' need for financial assistance would be greater than that of the defendant employer. The Supreme Court has ruled that district courts may exercise their discretion in awarding attorneys' fees to prevailing defendants. However, the Court explained, such an award must be based on a finding that the plaintiff's charge was "frivolous, unreasonable or without foundation." (*Christiansburg Garment Co. v. EEOC*)

Attorneys' fees are much more likely to be awarded when the successful party is a plaintiff. Thus, one court of appeals decided that an employer's good faith does not preclude a back pay award (*Clark v. American Marine Corp.*), and another held that attorneys' fees can be awarded even though the defendant did not pursue frivolous arguments (*Robinson v. P. Lorillard Co.*) and that they may be awarded to parties not primarily interested in employment but rather in attacking the employer's employment policies. (*Lea v. Cone Mills Corp.*)

The Supreme Court issued the following pronouncement on the computation of attorneys' fees: The most useful starting point for determining the amount of reasonable fees is the number of hours reasonably expended on litigation multiplied by a reasonable hourly rate, since this calculation provides an objective basis on which to make initial estimates of the value of services.

The Court also said that an attorney for a plaintiff who has obtained excellent results should recover a fully compensatory fee, which normally would encompass all hours reasonably expended, but might include a fee enhancement for exceptional success. And, the Court explained, an award should not be reduced simply because a plaintiff failed to prevail on every contention raised. (*Hensley v. Eckerhart*)

In *Johnson v. Georgia Highway Express*, an appeals court listed the following factors as determinative:

- The time and labor required of the lawyers
- The difficulty of the questions in the case

- The skill required to perform the legal service
- The other employment lost by the attorney due to acceptance of the case
- The customary fee
- Whether the fee is fixed or contingent
- Time limitations imposed by the client
- The amount of money involved and the results obtained
- The experience, reputation, and ability of the attorneys
- The desirability of the case
- The lawyer's relationship with the client
- Awards in similar cases

However, another court of appeals said that a formula was necessary to translate the 12-factor analysis set forth in *Johnson* into dollars and cents.

The U.S. Court of Appeals for the District of Columbia stated that the "lodestar" attorneys' fee, which is based on hours spent and hourly rate, may be adjusted up or down to reflect unusually good or bad representation, taking into account the level of skill expected of the attorney. Therefore, the court explained, there may be more than one reasonable rate for each attorney who represented successful plaintiffs and for each kind of work involved in the suit. (*Copeland v. Marshall*)

TEMPORARY INJUNCTIVE RELIEF

Under the 1972 amendments, the EEOC and the attorney general are given the authority to seek temporary injunctive relief to preserve the status quo where there is an allegation of unlawful retaliatory action. But this amendment did not take away the pre-existing right of an employee to seek such an injunction on his or her own where the employee believes he or she is the victim of retaliatory action, an appeals court has held. (*Drew v. Liberty Mutual Insurance Co.*)

15
TITLE VII: REPORTS

Under Section 709(c) of Title VII, the EEOC has authority to require covered employers, employment agencies, labor unions, state and local governments, school districts, and institutions of higher education to keep and preserve records and to file reports. In addition, Section 709(a) of Title VII gives the EEOC access to, and the right to copy, any "evidence" of a person proceeded against or investigated. But the right to copy is limited to evidence that related to proscribed unfair employment practices and is relevant to a charge under investigation by the EEOC.

There are provisions for granting exemptions from the recordkeeping and reporting requirements in cases of undue hardship. There are also statutory exemptions established for those required to keep records or file reports under a state or local law or an executive order. It is unlawful for the EEOC to make public any information from the required records.

In addition to giving the EEOC the authority to require the filing of reports, Title VII authorizes it to require the posting of a prescribed notice setting forth summaries of pertinent provisions of the 1964 Civil Rights Act and information related to the filing of a complaint.

The EEOC requires an employer to keep for at least six months all personnel records that are made. The records that must be kept are those made in connection with job applicants, hiring, promotion, demotion, transfer, layoffs, rates of pay and other forms of compensation, and selection for apprenticeship or training. If an employee is discharged, the employer must keep his or her personnel records for six months from the date of discharge.

Generally, employers may acquire the information on racial or ethnic identity by visual survey of the work force or by keeping post-employment records. Eliciting information on the race/ethnic identity of an employee by direct inquiry is not encouraged. The EEOC recommends that records on an employee's race/ethnic identity be kept separately from the employee's personnel file or from other records available to those responsible for personnel decisions.

REPORT FORMS REQUIRED

The EEOC has seven forms that must be filed:

- *EEO-1* must be filed by all employers covered by Title VII that have 100 or more employees and by government contractors covered by Executive Order 11246 that have 50 or more employees and government contracts of $50,000 or more.
- *EEO-2* must be filed annually by joint labor-management committees that have five or more trainees in their programs and at least one employer having 25 or more employees and one union sponsor having 25 or more members covered by Title VII.
- *EEO-2-E* must be filed annually by every establishment with 25 or more employees by each employer who (1) has a total company-wide employment of 100 or more employees, (2) conducts and controls an employer-operated apprenticeship program, and (3) has five or more apprentices in the establishment.
- *EEO-3* must be filed annually by local unions that have had 100 or more members at any time since the previous December 31. An international union is not required to file a report unless it operated a local union under a trusteeship or other arrangement or performs any functions of a local.
- *EEO-4* must be filed annually by state and local governmental jurisdictions with 100 or more employees.
- *EEO-5* must be filed by every public elementary and secondary school system or district, including every individually or separately administered district within a

system, and every separately administered school with 100 or more employees. In addition, selected schools with 15 or more employees will be required to file the form biannually, with the determination of which schools are being selected being the responsibility of the School Reporting Committee.

- *EEO-6* must be filed every two years by every institution of higher learning with 15 or more employees.

RECORDS REQUIRED

The records that must be kept by employers include the following:

- All personnel records that are made (But an employer need not keep application forms and other pre-employment records of applicants for seasonal or temporary jobs.)
- A copy of the employer report form (EEO-1) that was filed most recently
- Post-employment records (When such records are kept, the EEOC suggests that they be kept separate from basic personnel records, and they may be incorporated in an automatic data processing system in the payroll department.)
- A list of applicants who wish to participate in apprenticeship programs. The list must be kept in the chronological order in which the applications are received. It should also include the address of each applicant and a notation of sex and identification of race or national origin. The list must be kept for two years or the period of a successful applicant's apprenticeship, whichever is longer.

Union Records

All local unions with 100 or more members must make and keep records that are necessary for completing EEOC report form EEO-3. These records must be kept for one year from the due date of the report. "Referral" unions must preserve other membership or referral records, including applications, for six months from the date of the making of the record.

STATE AND LOCAL GOVERNMENTS

Under the 1972 amendments, state and local jurisdictions with 100 or more employees are required to file annually form EEO-4 covering employment by minority group, sex, occupation, and salary range. The EEOC's right to require states to submit these forms has been upheld by a circuit court. *(United States v. New Hampshire)*

There also are record-keeping rules for elementary and secondary schools and institutions of higher education. Under EEOC rules, public and secondary school systems, districts, and individual schools with 15 or more employees must keep personnel and employment records for two years and employment statistics by race and job category for three years. All public or private institutions of higher education with 15 or more employees must keep records necessary for filing form EEO-6, whether or not they are required to file the report.

16
ENFORCEMENT OF OTHER EEO LAWS

Enforcement of the Age Discrimination in Employment Act (ADEA) and the Equal Pay Act is the responsibility of the EEOC. Enforcement of federal contractor requirements is the responsibility of the Department of Labor and the OFCCP. Federal employee EEO requirements are enforced by the EEOC. All of these are discussed below.

TRANSFER OF ADEA, EPA TO THE EEOC

President Carter transferred authority over the ADEA and the Equal Pay Act from the Labor Department to the EEOC. That transfer authority was found in the Reorganization Act of 1977, which contained a one-house legislative veto. Subsequently, the Supreme Court decided in an immigration case that this type of veto authority violated the U.S. Constitution. One court of appeals has upheld the transfer of authority of the Equal Pay Act to the EEOC *(EEOC v. Hernando Bank)*, but another court of appeals has invalidated the transfer of authority of the ADEA and ruled that only the Department of Labor could bring such suits. *(EEOC v. CBS, Inc.)*

AGE DISCRIMINATION IN EMPLOYMENT ACT

Responsibility for enforcing the Age Discrimination in Employment Act was transferred from the Wage-Hour Division of the Labor Department to the EEOC, effective July 1, 1979. Ad-

147

ministrative and enforcement activities under the Act, formerly assumed by the Secretary of Labor, are now delegated to the EEOC, and include the following:

- The EEOC has the power to make investigations and to require that employers keep records in accordance with the provisions of the Act.
- An aggrieved individual must file a charge with the EEOC within 180 days of an alleged act of discrimination. In a case which is the subject of state litigation, the charge must be filed with the EEOC within 300 days after the act complained of or within 30 days of receipt of notice of termination of proceedings under state law.
- Before any court action may begin under the Act, the EEOC is required to attempt conciliation between the parties. During this period of conciliation, for up to one year, the statue of limitations is tolled.
- The Act authorizes jury trial of any issue of fact in the case, regardless of whether equitable relief is being sought. Damages over and above back pay and other job-related benefits may be awarded only if the complainant can show that the employer's violation was "willful."

The EEOC issued its own ADEA interpretations in September 1981 (401 FEP Manual 331), which basically parallel those issued by the Department's Wage and Hour Administration.

EQUAL PAY ACT

When the EEOC assumed enforcement responsibility for the Equal Pay Act from the Department of Labor on July 1, 1979, it declined to adopt the Wage and Hour Administrator's Interpretative Bulletin on the Act, but noted that until it issued its own interpretations, employers may continue to rely on existing interpretations, and opinions of the Wage and Hour Administrator to the extent that they are not inconsistent with statutory revisions and judicial interpretations. On September 1, 1981, the EEOC published proposed interpretive regulations on the Equal Pay Act (401 FEP Manual 325), which, when finally adopted, will supersede those of the Wage and Hour Administrator.

Investigators from the EEOC exploring a possible violation of the Act may enter an establishment, inspect the premises and records, transcribe records, and interview employees. According to the Act, investigators will then "advise employers regarding any changes necessary or desirable regarding payroll, recordkeeping, and other personnel practices which will aid in achieving and maintaining compliance with the law."

FEDERAL CONTRACTOR REQUIREMENTS

Enforcement procedures differ for executive orders, the Vocational Rehabilitation Act, and the Vietnam Era Veterans' Readjustment Assistance Act.

Executive Orders

Executive Order 11246 on equal employment opportunity for employees of federal government contractors is enforced by the Department of Labor and its Office of Federal Contract Compliance Programs with the cooperation of the contracting agencies and departments within the federal government.

Under the Executive Order, the Secretary of Labor is given the power to

- Publish the names of noncomplying contractors or unions
- Recommend suits by the Justice Department to compel compliance
- Recommend action by the EEOC or the Justice Department for furnishing false information
- Cancel the contract of a noncomplying employer
- Debar a noncomplying employer from future government contract work until it has demonstrated a willingness to comply

The threat of contract cancellation or debarment from future government contract work is the major weapon in the government's arsenal under the Executive Order.

Federal contract compliance authority for equal employment opportunity and affirmative action was consolidated in OFCCP under Executive Order 12086, effective October 8, 1978. The Order eliminated the assigned contract compliance functions of 11 other federal agencies. In a related action, the OFCCP has assigned contract compliance monitoring in its regional offices on a geographical basis rather than on the previous industry basis.

In enforcing Executive Order 11246, the OFCCP has placed primary emphasis on compliance reviews and pre-award programs that cover the entire employment program of a contractor or subcontractor, rather than on encouraging individual complaints of noncompliance. Although machinery exists for processing complaints, the OFCCP is primarily concerned with broader compliance efforts.

Pre-award reviews or surveys of low bidders are conducted on formally advertised supply contracts amounting to $1 million or more. To qualify for the award of the contract, the bidder must be able to show in the pre-award review that it is able to comply with the equal employment opportunity mandate. To establish standards for reviewing affirmative action program of government contractors, the OFCCP issued Revised Order No. 4 (401 FEP Manual 2831). The Order provides for a compliance review of nonconstruction contractors or subcontractors with 50 or more employees and a contract for more than $50,000.

Affirmative Action Requirements—Under Order No. 4, government contractors are required to develop written affirmative action plans containing the following:

- An analysis of all major job classifications, with an explanation of any "underutilization" of minorities in any of the job classes
- Goals and targets and affirmative action commitments designed to relieve any deficiencies (But the Order specifies that a contractor's compliance will not be judged by reviewing the contents of the program, the extent of the contractor's adherence to it, and the contractor's good-faith efforts to make its program work toward realization of the goals within timetables set for completion.)

The guidelines under Order No. 4 also outline suggested procedures for use in establishing, implementing, and judging an acceptable affirmative action program. The contractor must consider such factors as these:

- Minority population of the labor area surrounding the facility and the size of the minority unemployment force
- General availability of minorities having requisite skills in the immediate labor area and in an area in which the contractor can reasonably recruit
- Availability of promotable minority employees within the contractor's organization
- Anticipated expansion, contraction, and turnover in the labor force
- Existence of institutions capable of training minorities in the requisite skills
- Degree of training which the contractor is reasonably able to undertake as a means of making all job classes available to minorities

The written programs "must relate to all major job categories at the facility with explanations if minorities or women are currently being underutilized." Where there are deficiencies, goals and timetables are required to utilize minorities and women at all levels and in all segments of the work force.

Compliance Reviews—Compliance reviews are undertaken in a series of steps. The procedure is as follows:

- First, the contractor receives a request from the OFCCP for a copy of the affirmative action plan to be forwarded to the compliance officer.
- If the compliance officer determines that the affirmative action program is inadequate, he or she may conduct an onsite inspection of the plant. The compliance officer is not required to notify the contractor of the date of the inspection.
- During an on-site review, the compliance officer may ask such questions as the following: How has the contractor sought to establish its EEO image in the community? Does the contractor use institutional as well as

recruitment advertising? Is an EEO reference included in advertising? And are lower level supervisors disseminating the EEO policy?

Self-monitoring—The OFCCP has established a national self-monitoring report system (NSMRS) that exempts contractors from compliance reviews for the duration of the agreement, if certain required "trend" reports do not turn up discrimination. AT&T, IBM, Hewlett-Packard, and General Motors are participants in the national self-monitoring program.

Back Pay, Penalties—Enforcement procedures and penalties are more stringent under the executive orders for government contractors than they are for employers generally under Title VII.

An employer found to have violated the orders may be debarred from government contracts. The OFCCP may place the contractor on an ineligible list circulated to the procurement agencies. Moreover, the right of the federal government to seek back pay from a contractor charged with discriminatory employment practices under Executive Order 11246 has been upheld. (*United States v. Duquesne Light Co.*)

Vocational Rehabilitation Act

Failure by a contractor or subcontractor to comply with Section 503 regulations may result in judicial enforcement, debarment from future government contracts, contract termination, or withholding of contract payments "as necessary to correct any violations." Each covered employer must maintain records on complaints, compliance reviews, and other required reports for one year. Affirmative action programs must be brought up to date annually.

Any applicant or employee may file a complaint alleging a violation with the Department of Labor. The charge must be filed within 180 days of the date of the alleged violation. If the employer and the complainant are unable to resolve the problem within 60 days, the Department procedures go into effect.

Under these procedures, the Labor Department investigates the complaints and attempts to obtain compliance by the employer "through conciliation and persuasion within a reasonable time." If the informal means are unsuccessful in resolving the violation, the contractor is given the opportunity for a formal hearing. The hearing officer makes recommendations, and final action will be taken by the OFCCP.

Vietnam Era Veterans' Act

Enforcement of the Vietnam Era Veterans' Readjustment Assistance Act is by complaint. If a person believes he or she has been discriminated against by a contractor, he or she may file a complaint with the Department of Labor. The Secretary of Labor is required to take such action as is consistent with the terms of the contract and the laws and regulations administered by the Department.

FEDERAL EMPLOYEE REQUIREMENTS

On January 1, 1979, as part of President Carter's plan to reorganize the federal civil rights program, responsibility for enforcing equal opportunity in federal employment was transferred from the U.S. Civil Service Commission (CSC) to the EEOC, although some responsibilities in this area rest with other agencies as noted below. The EEOC has adopted certain Civil Service Commission regulations with respect to equal employment opportunity in the federal government.

Under further provisions of the Carter reorganization, the CSC was replaced by the Office of Personnel Management (OPM), which has responsibility for personnel management in the federal sector. The OPM has issued Federal Equal Opportunity Recruitment Program regulations (401 FEP Manual 1161) and guidelines (401 FEP Manual 1166) designed to provide effective standards for enforcement of government-wide recruitment policies to eliminate underrepresentation of minorities and women in civil service employment.

In addition, a three-member Merit Systems Protection Board (MSPB) took over the employee appeals functions of the old CSC. The MSPB has authority to hear federal employee complaints in "mixed" cases involving adverse personnel actions joined with allegations of discrimination. The MSPB decides both issues in such cases. However, employees may request the EEOC to reconsider any such decision and deadlocks between the two agencies are decided by a three-member panel. Employees also retain the option of filing a separate complaint in federal court.

Federal agencies and their components are required to establish "targeted recruitment programs" to remedy any "underrepresentation" of minorities and women in their employment ranks, under the OPM's "Federal Equal Recruitment Opportunity Program." Federal agencies and components must make underrepresentation determinations by comparing their own employment percentages for particular minority/sex groups with the groups' civilian labor force employment percentages. In most cases, local civilian labor force figures will be those for the "standard metropolitan statistical area" (SMSA) in which the agency is located.

TABLE OF CASES

A

AFSCME v. Washington (W. D. Wash, 1983) 578 F Supp 846, 33 FEP Cases 808   36

Abraham v. Graphic Arts Int'l Union (CA DC, 1981) 26 FEP Cases 818   32

Aikens v. United States Postal Serv. Bd. of Governors (1983) 460 US 711, 31 FEP Cases 609   84

Albemarle Paper Co. v. Moody (1975) 422 US 405, 10 FEP Cases 1181   138

Alexander v. Gardner-Denver Co. (1974) 415 US 36, 7 FEP Cases 81   11, 133

Allegheny-Ludlum Indus., Inc.; United States v. (CA 5, 1975) 517 F2d 826, 11 FEP Cases 167   127

Allen v. Lovejoy (CA 6, 1977) 533 F2d 522, 14 FEP Cases 1194   40

Allen v. United States Steel Corp. (CA 5, 1982) 665 F2d 689, 27 FEP Cases 1293   131

American Bank of Commerce; Hodgson v. (CA 5, 1971) 477 F2d 416, 9 FEP Cases 677   58

American Newspaper Publishers Ass'n v. Alexander (CA DC, 1969) 1 FEP Cases 703   39

American Nurses Ass'n (DC Ill, 1985) 606 F Supp 1313, 37 FEP Cases 705   362

American Tobacco Co. v. Patterson (1982) 456 US 63, 28 FEP Cases 713   106

Anderson v. General Dynamics, Convair Aerospace Div. (CA 9, 1978) 589 F2d 397, 17 FEP Cases 1644   53

Ansonia Bd. of Educ. v. Philbrook (1986) ____US____, 42 FEP Cases 359   49

Approved Personnel Serv., Inc.; Hodgson v. (CA 4, 1975) 529 F2d 760, 11 FEP Cases 688   63

Arizona Governing Comm. v. Norris (CA 9, 1986) 41 FEP Cases 820, on remand from (1983) 463 US 1073, 32 FEP Cases 233   37

Arline v. School Bd. of Nassau County (CA 11, 1985) 772 F2d 759, 39 FEP Cases 9   77

Asbestos Workers, Local 53 v. McCarty, Inc., see Vogler v. McCarty, Inc.

Ashton v. Civiletti (CA DC, 1979) 20 FEP Cases 1601   85

Atascadero State Hosp. v. Scanlon (1985) 473 US____, 38 FEP Cases 97   76

Ayon v. Sampson (CA 9, 1976) 547 F2d 446, 14 FEP Cases 149   85

B

Bailey Co.; EEOC v. (CA 6, 1977) 563 F2d 439, 15 FEP Cases 972   122

Baldwin County Welcome Center v. Brown (1984) 466 US 147, 34 FEP Cases 929   132

Barela v. United Nuclear Corp. (DC NM, 1970) 462 F2d 142, 4 FEP Cases 831   116

Barrett v. Omaha Nat'l Bank (CA 8, 1984) 726 F2d 424, 35 FEP Cases 593   34

Bazemore v. Friday (1986) 478 US____, 41 FEP Cases 92   104, 125

Behrens Drug Co.; Hodgson v. (CA 5, 1973) 475 F2d 1041, 9 FEP Cases 816   56

155

INDEX